HIS SUNRISE
MY SUNSET

A True Story
of Love and Loss

Jan Hurst

Trust in Him

Romans 15:13

Jan Hurst

Table of Contents

Introduction

$\mathcal{L}$ ife is unpredictable for all of us. We may be the strongest of planners, but we are not able to control outside forces in this world of free will. The loss of a spouse is one of the most significant life changes we face. Each phase of life brings good and bad side effects, but widowhood is one of the devastating and humbling times that we struggle to accept. We each have our own unique, individual situation and personal style for dealing with adversities. The impact of complex family dynamics and personalities magnify as we walk through crises. The loss of a husband leaves a wife to deal with the family, finances, property, and legal responsibilities. Until we actually become a widow, the demands are not clear. People usually surprise us even when we think they are predictable. Family and friends are people, and people can be unforeseen.

Finding yourself alone truly tests your faith. If you have a relationship with Jesus, trauma can draw you closer. If you don't have a relationship, dramatic challenges can help open your eyes to a new life if you let it. Tragedy often causes us to pause and think about what we believe because we know we need something. Our experience convinced me how important it is to think of everyday as possibly our last. We don't know what will happen tomorrow or even today. But we do know how we have lived. We should live today as if we won't have tomorrow. I have had confirmation about that.

This is the story of how quickly a life can change, without warning, even when we think our marriage has reached its peak. During the stages of change, the incredible mind games take over to remind us of highlights and lowlights of our marriage. Constant flashbacks of memories are shared to convey the feelings of confusion and the rollercoaster ride of emotions. Maybe our story will help someone to appreciate their own story more. Maybe our story will help someone to ask serious questions about their own beliefs.

Dedication

I dedicate this book to my precious husband, Steve. Life is such a complex and unpredictable experience as we stumble through without a copy of God's plan for our individual purpose. I still don't know the rest of my life story or understand my planned purpose, but I do believe my life with Steve was no accident. We were simply two imperfect people who fit perfectly together. Steve was the love of my life. We married young and grew up together. I miss him so very much, as does our family. I know he is waiting for me, and I look forward to being reunited. Faith held us together from the time we joined under God, and faith will be my safety line until I rejoin him.

I thank God for my Steve and all he was to me and our family. Steve was a special husband, dad, grandpa, and son. He expected nothing from anyone but gave so much. We were so blessed to have such wonderful daughters and their families and Steve's stepmother. They were there through the toughest of times. My love and gratitude to my family as well as the special friends who have been there for me and with me.

**Steve was so happy at the delivery of his
2010 Corvette Grand Sport.**

1

In an Instant

riday, the 13th of August, 2010, began as a beautiful day filled with warm and tender gestures by a husband I loved dearly. He was being so very sweet. We had retired months earlier and started executing plans to enjoy traveling and meeting friends as we explored the United States, especially joining Corvette caravans. Corvettes were Steve's passion and, as his wife, it was a large part of my life. We had a great time traveling and just being together in the car for hours. While some might find that unattractive, I found it to be wonderful quality time with the most important person in my life, whether we were chatting or perfectly silent.

We had spent the night in Bowling Green, Kentucky, leaving the hotel before seven that morning, headed to meet a caravan at the National Corvette Museum. We looked forward to driving as part of the miles of Corvettes following each other on a fun adventure to Indiana, ending up at a spectacular resort. Steve was in a particularly good mood and such a gentleman. He opened my car door and handed me a card. The card declared his continued love after so many years. What a romantic morning this was. He told me he really wanted to renew our vows for the fourth time. We girls dream of men who will shower us with such sweet affection because we often lack it. I had lacked it for many years, but now he was back, as romantic as he had ever been.

Steve and I had been together long enough to have enjoyed the peaks of "lovey dovey" times and the valleys of everyday practical life. Steve had been more practical most of the years. Diamonds and such were not practical to him. As teenagers, our daughters had once badgered their dad, asking him, "Why don't you buy Mom a big diamond ring?" to which he replied, "What would she do with it if she had one?" "Wear it!" they almost shouted. He had given me a diamond engagement ring—but its size fit a young airman's budget. While diamonds had never been a priority for either of us, I must say that I was a real girl. There's nothing wrong with having one if you can afford it!

Steve was fairly quiet unless you mentioned cars, the Air Force, or his girls. He was an easy going, rather modest kind of guy, who appreciated his family but didn't talk a lot. He was always busy, working in the yard, helping in the house, or washing and waxing cars when he was home. He had been good at encouraging people at work as part of his management style but seemed to think if we lived with him, we must know how he felt. He would hug his girls and show he loved them, but it might follow a warning, "Look out!" preempting a little punch to the arm. I guess you might call it guy affection. If I whined that I needed to hear him say he loved me, his comment was, "I told you I loved you when I married you, so until further notice, I love you." He was joking, but I doubt he realized how it stung to hear that. It wasn't until the latter years that he became more comfortable about sharing his feelings.

Steve had become more emotional and expressive as we got older. Not only did he surprise me with real diamonds, but he had started buying greeting cards. He bought cards to share his feelings and to insert typed notes with further personalization. I believe two factors contributed to that. He had been diagnosed with Parkinson's in 2005, and my mother had died of a stroke in January, 2009. His symptoms were gradually getting worse and Steve was smacked by feeling his mortality when my mother suddenly died. Besides requiring increased doses of medicine that affected his emotions, he was experiencing heightened frustration over a body ignoring his commands.

Parkinson's is a disorder of the nervous system that affects movement, including tremors and various other degenerative symptoms. Both of our dads had been diagnosed with Parkinson's years earlier, within a year of each other. My dad was ten years younger than Steve's but was not as healthy. Steve shared his dad's strong heart and good health. He had always lived the military practice of disciplined exercise and was used to feeling well. He was shocked watching his dad deteriorate from the ravages of such a greedy disease as it took over his body. Being of good health, his dad had the sad fate of living with Parkinson's to the gruesome end. Steve dreaded thinking that could be his fate.

My dad, on the other hand, experienced advancing symptoms of the disease but did not reach the end stages before congestive heart failure took his life. Having been a heavy smoker since his early teens, he had not enjoyed such a clean health record. Steve viewed my dad's heart failure as a blessing, even though my dad died when he was seventy-nine, and his dad had lived to be eighty-six. He did not want to live to stages of total dependency, slowly and painfully dying as his body continued to fail him. Although he spoke of it little, there was no doubt it remained on his mind.

We had just bought a new 2010 Corvette months before this trip. Although he really wanted the new Grand Sport, he knew the time was coming when he would be unable to drive and didn't want to spend the money. It wasn't practical. I convinced him that because one day he would lose the privilege of driving, he should have the car while he could still drive safely. He asked me in a teasing tone if I would drive him around in it when he could no longer drive. Because he always insisted on driving, that was an inside joke of sorts that was also admission of reality. Steve very much thought the man of the house should drive whenever possible, and the practice worked for me. I rather enjoyed feeling taken care of with a husband who liked to handle the driving, leaving me to enjoy the sights around me.

Buying this Corvette was similar to the first one we bought in 1990. Steve learned to drive on a Corvette before he was of driving age and never got over it. His parents divorced, and he never saw the car again. He always wanted one. I promised him if he would retire from the Air Force, I would buy him one. He retired July 1, 1990, and on July 26, we were at a car dealer to test drive a Corvette. We drove a coupe around a few minutes and pulled back into the dealer, parking next to a red convertible with a white top. Steve said, "*That* is a Corvette—a *real* Corvette." He said you really needed a red convertible with a white top. So, I told the salesman we wanted to see it. He explained that the car had actually been sold a few weeks earlier, but the guy never came to pick it up, so he would see if it was available. Sure enough, the buyer had backed out of the deal, and it was for sale. We took it for a drive, and Steve was just beaming. When we got back to the dealer, the salesman asked if he wanted to write it up and drive it home. Steve said, "I love it, but a convertible just isn't practical. We still need to shop for groceries and stuff." I looked at him and said, "Steve, buying a Corvette is not practical! Do you want the car? You have always wanted one so get what you want."

We bought the red Corvette convertible with the white top. He was so happy, he was giddy. I had to talk him into it, but I was extremely happy for him. That night he could not sleep. He kept going out to the garage and sitting in the car.

The next morning, he exclaimed, "We have to take the car back. It just is not practical." I refused to return it, and he was thrilled! He was as practical with himself as he was with me or the girls, yet he was generous.

As he mellowed over the years, he had loosened up a good bit about conserving money by the time we bought this fourth Corvette coupe in stunning blue. We could afford a new car, having always been conservative. We did not buy beyond our means. Yes, we spent money on cars, but we didn't drink or smoke or gamble or spend on other money-burning activities. Since our daughters had gotten through college and married, we had been sincere about tithing first, saving second, supporting some charities, and then enjoying some of our money. Our family was raised, and we had come full circle back to where we started with just the two of us. When he finally agreed that the new car would be a lot of fun, and he really, really desired it, his guilt subsided. That August day as we left the hotel, he kept saying over and over how he loved the car and how much it meant to him that I wanted him to have it. He said, as he had many times, how he felt like he did when we first got together, and he was so, so happy. We were enjoying a high point of our lives. We were retired and had nothing but fun adventures to look forward to together.

We were excited to join the caravan and were close to our turnoff when we heard and felt a kind of thump. It was nothing at all dramatic. I said rather matter-of-factly, "What did we hit?" to which he responded calmly while trying to control the car, "I don't know." In an instant the car was careening right into a guardrail. Fortunately, I was left with that as my only memory. A guardrail was seemingly coming at us and then nothing—

An eighteen-wheel tanker truck changed lanes right into our driver side rear wheel. We were going seventy miles an hour in the right lane of a three-lane interstate highway. We were thrown into a spinout at that high rate of speed.

The truck started to pass us, but the driver could not see us below the big truck cab as he changed lanes. The lady in the car behind us said she couldn't believe the truck put on his blinker and turned right into us. Because it was about 7 a.m., and the truck was from Ohio, I can only guess he'd driven all night, was tired, and forgot we were there. I know he could not see our car when he hit us, but I believe he would have seen us before. We had been on the highway in the right lane for a couple of miles. Steve was not passing him on the right. In fact, I don't think Steve was that aware of him. Morning traffic was whizzing by, and the expectation was that drivers would stay in their lane. We had no idea what had happened. I choose not to dwell on the why of the event or what he might have been doing. I would hate to think he was on the phone or texting at that moment. I just know we were involved in a horrific accident that morning.

The result was our car flipping on the guardrail, the top of our car ripped off, and landing in a field, right side up, facing the highway and the mangled guardrail. The windshield was shattered and practically laying in our laps. The windshield wipers were rapidly swishing broken glass like confetti everywhere. I guess we both were unconscious briefly because I only remember coming to and thinking, "My goodness, we had an accident." I had a flashback of having been hit by a drunk some thirty years earlier when I was left with significant injuries. I felt a sensation of being in a dreamlike state. Surely this had to be a horrible dream, I thought. But, then I realized I was awake, and we really were in our car.

I tried to look over at Steve and immediately saw that he wasn't okay. He was slumped down, lying against his seat, bleeding, the white bone of his skull fully exposed. I gently put his scalp back down from where it was sticking up to try to cover the exposure and bleeding. Almost immediately, the lady that was driving right behind us stopped and ran down to our car. She offered me her scarf to put on Steve's head, which she helped me do, being careful not to move him. Then Gary, a friend from the museum who was scheduled to lead the caravan, saw our car and also pulled off. Steve had regained consciousness and asked what happened. Just as I was telling him I did not know what happened, I heard the truck driver calling out as he stood at the guardrail looking down at us. He was very distraught saying over and over, "I'm sorry. I didn't see you." I then saw his truck pulled off the road where he'd stopped. I told Steve we had been hit by a truck.

Steve recognized Gary when he leaned in on his side of the car. He frantically asked him, "Was this my fault?" Gary assured him it was not his fault and there was nothing he could have done to avoid it. Gary reached over to shut the car off. It had not occurred to me as I sat still buckled in and totally focused on Steve. I didn't even realize the top was gone even though people were talking to me without a roof or windshield between us. When they asked me if we rolled, I couldn't tell them. The whole incident happened so quickly, and I was so stunned that it felt unreal. I just wanted to wake up!

Meantime, the truck driver stood there and waited to talk to police when they arrived. I could faintly see him standing in front of the guardrail as he kept saying he didn't see us. He was clearly shaken. I forgave him, which I found odd when I later thought about it. I don't know why I thought that right then, except my sense was that he didn't hit us on purpose, yet here we were. Besides, who cared what happened or who caused it? All that mattered was getting help for Steve. I ached but I did not feel as though I was seriously hurt. Steve, on the other hand, immediately complained that he couldn't feel his feet or hands! An emergency crew was on the scene within a few minutes, and by that time Steve was complaining he couldn't get enough air.

Steve was immobilized and carefully lifted into the ambulance, and then I was handled the same way. I told them my shoulder was mainly what hurt but the EMT said, "I can see your car. Do not try to move. We will get you out." I remember the police asking if we had seat belts on, and the EMT told him we were still locked in and they had to release the belts for us. In my foggy state of mind, I remember looking for OnStar and seeing the wires hanging down on the floor because the rearview mirror was gone, and things were just dangling. I felt grateful that witnesses and EMT had come so quickly because I was not able to call for help. I had a fleeting thought about how awful it would have been had we been on a deserted road some place.

A strange calmness enveloped me, convincing me a guardian angel must be with us. I was not panicked or scared, curiously. Somehow, I felt God knew what was happening, and we were being cared for. I know we were taught that, but at this moment I could feel an indescribable presence I never felt before. I recall asking Gary to get my purse, of all things to think of. I guess a purse just becomes part of a girl's dress, so we feel lost without it.

We lay awkwardly on backboards side-by-side in the ambulance. Steve was struggling to breathe but managed to ask about me. The EMT put my hand on his and told him I was right there with him, and I was holding his hand. Steve said, "I can't feel it." I assured him that our hands were together, and I was right there. It seemed barely a few minutes before we arrived at the emergency entrance. They told us that I was going to be taken into the emergency room, and Steve was going to be airlifted to Nashville to the trauma center. Steve said, "I love you," with what little breath he had. I replied, "I love you." Then I was whisked inside, and the ambulance sped off to the heliport pad. My heart raced as I tried to quietly pray for Steve while fighting off negative thoughts about how he was. I wanted to know how he was! I don't think I said much other than answering questions, but my mind was racing in circles. Lying still while scans and X-rays were done became a mammoth task. Of great inconvenience was acid reflux raging as I was forced to lie there for hours.

Gary had stayed to talk to police and make sure our car was towed away and taken to a safe place. Then he and his wife came to the emergency room where I was being thoroughly examined to identify any injuries. I felt so very fortunate to have them with me and thinking for me as they started working to contact our daughters. I don't recall too much about the details, but I do remember them getting connected with Michele and Terri. Michele, our first daughter, had just visited us at our home in Tyler, Texas. We had shared dinner with her the night before. She was on her way back to Syracuse, New York, where she and her husband, Jonathan, are neonatologists and have three children. Her younger sister, Terri, was in Tyler where she and her husband, Ken, are attorneys with two children. Our daughters dropped everything and immediately started driving to Nashville, where their dad was taken.

After the doctors determined my main injury was a sprained shoulder, they released me and Wendell, another friend from the museum, took me to get prescriptions and pick up luggage from our car, so he could finally drive me to Nashville. Having discovered I could not see Steve because he was in surgery, I decided to take the medicine and rest until the girls could get there. I was not feeling too well by then. The adrenalin was slowing a bit, I suspect. My shoulder was quite painful and aches had taken over my body. I just wanted to lie down. I told Wendell I would be fine, and he should drive back to Bowling Green, but he waited in the lobby until Michele showed up. It hurt to think and my mind flittered all over, but I was aware of Gary and Wendell caring for us. Late that night, Wendell finally allowed himself to drive home after he had taken us to dinner and we had been to the hospital. Gary and Wendell were certainly special guardians that day, and I sensed some unexplainable presence. I have sometimes wondered how angels appear. I am convinced there must have been at least one angel with us.

When the girls and I were finally able to see Steve, it was unnerving. He had the full halo bolted into his head, and his scalp was a patchwork quilt of stitches sewing it back together. We had not been able to see him sooner because of all the surgery he required. He had a tracheotomy done in the helicopter and was on a respirator. He had fractured C1 through C5 vertebrae and had a complete spinal cord injury. He was receiving medicine to keep his heart functioning, and because he was now a quadriplegic, his body was swelling unmercifully without circulation. His hands looked and felt like gloves that were blown up and stretched to the max — so eerie to see or touch.

I was shocked at the sight of my strong hunk of a man with that massive cage contraption on his head, a roadmap of stitches holding his scalp together, and him lying so prone with machines making his body function. Steve looked so wilted. I tried to imagine how helpless, confused, and hurt he must have felt. Though he hated medicine and hospitals, he had been stripped of having any control. He was in his least favorite place, totally at the mercy of others. At the same time, I imagined that he might not feel or understand much. He had been through such severe trauma and was heavily medicated.

The medical team met with us, explaining in detail how serious the injuries were. I was overwhelmed. My head was whirling, and my heart was racing. I kept thinking over and over about how I would take care of him when I got him home because he would be like Steve Reeves after his accident. His condition was similar. However, our Steve was sixty-five and had Parkinson's, as the doctor kept reminding me. Still, I rationalized that he was so healthy and because we lived next door to Terri, I would somehow be able to manage. We had a one-story house built with walk-in showers, based on expectations of having my mother live with us after my dad died. Being a rather organized planner by nature, I was already seeking information about possibilities for care and necessary medical equipment.

Looking back, I can see how unrealistically I was dreaming. I had no idea how very intense and difficult it would be to care for a quadriplegic or where to start such an endeavor. How I respect people who have been dedicated caretakers. At the time, I did not question that I would somehow learn what to do and find a way to take care of him. Somehow we would make this work. I was raised that way. I wanted to care for him.

Being raised as an Air Force dependent, my dad was always pushing me to adjust to whatever came my way. Because we moved so frequently, whenever I raised a complaint, he would firmly declare, "You have to adjust because life isn't fair, and the world is not going to adjust for you." I grew up knowing I would hear that if I protested, so I learned not to. I also developed an internal mechanism that allowed me to shift my attitude when things did not go my way. I would do whatever I could to make the best of situations and accept what I was given in life. I thank my dad for consistently holding me accountable for myself. Reflection tells me that because of that "skill" to adjust, I have survived and sometimes excelled through many difficult challenges. I guess most of us like to feel some control over our lives, but my dad prepared me to take the lumps and find a different way. With Steve unable to function on his own, I would find some path to take care of him. We would be fine, I thought; I hoped; I prayed.

Steve was in a trauma center where a huge room was full of elaborately equipped beds with only curtains separating them. The reason was the urgency of care required for these patients, many victims of motorcycle and automobile accidents. Only two visitors at a time were allowed with the patient during the limited visiting hours. I knew the girls each needed their time with their dad as much as I did, so I traded off visitation time with them, as difficult as it was to leave him. My minutes with him flew by.

Steve surely liked time with his two girls together. They were always the light of his life. He was so proud of them. Funny how our unanswered desires can sometimes turn out so well. Steve wanted to have a boy so badly. When I was pregnant, he always referred to the baby as "he" or "him" until our two girls emerged. I had a friend at the time I was pregnant with Terri that was from a family of seven girls and finally a boy as the eighth child. We talked about the obvious possibility of having another girl. (Sonograms were not done that long ago, so you had the excitement of a surprise at the time of birth.) We agreed no matter how many babies we had, there was a 50/50 chance of having a boy every time. Our rationalization was that we needed to decide how many children we wanted. We started out, before we had one baby, flippantly saying we wanted four children. But with baby number two facing us, we decided that we preferred two children to three girls. We were not having babies until a boy appeared!

As it turned out, Steve adored his girls so much. I thought about that day when Terri was born. Steve brought flowers for me with a card that read, "I love all three of my girls!" He never brought up having a boy again because he didn't care. He had two heathy baby girls, and that was all that mattered. The bonus was how much he enjoyed them as they grew up and how proud he was of who they became. He discovered girls are fun, too, and he could do sports with them. He also found out how little girls have a special spot in their hearts for their daddy. No doubt, the minutes his girls spent visiting with him were precious to him.

Any time away from him dragged and dragged, making the day very long, since we could only be with him such few hours a day. I just wanted to be there with him and see for myself how he was. Steve and I were back to having just each other since our girls started their own families. Like most families, our lives surrounded the girl's activities when they were home. I think we remained fairly close with our girls, but we always wanted them to feel independence and freedom that we felt denied growing up, so though we kept in touch, we left them alone. We allowed them to decide when they wanted us around. We didn't call all the time or keep up with their details of daily life. But we always wanted to make sure they knew we were there for them no matter what they needed or why. We tried to share unconditional love, especially because we both had desired that so much ourselves. We were so proud of them. We knew they needed to have their families their way, and we knew their way would be great.

We depended on each other. We both had always been more content being home than socializing, and the inclination heightened once we retired. We shared a dislike for political groups at work and were shy about social gatherings. Neither of us drank, and most social events with coworkers had centered around drinking. Neither of us fit into good old boy work environments. Both of us strove to be examples of high integrity and extended our help to others, especially as bosses at work, to make the best of whatever operations we led. We enjoyed helping people develop and find their best fit in a job, but we moved often enough that we had no lifelong friends. Besides, we both had been in management, and friendships tend to be different when you are the boss.

We both had experienced betrayal by people we mentored, which only resurfaced our trust issues, drawing us more into our protective cocoon with each other. Relying on each other was our only safe haven. Consequently, our days were spent doing things together, if only working around the house or yard. After all these years, we still liked to just be together. We felt comfort merely by being with each other. We didn't have to talk all the time. We were fairly active with church and had started regularly praying together years earlier after joining a church that led us to personally study the Bible. After years of attending church, we had learned how to become engaged at church. How I longed to pray out loud with Steve, but he was unable to speak. I longed to talk with him, period. I was used to making decisions with him, not about him.

Michele, Terri, and I spent some of our "free" time in the large main lobby downstairs and visited the chapel frequently. Steve required so much care. We knew the nurses were busy working on him all the while we waited. I had spoken to Herb, our Sunday Morning Bible Study teacher in Tyler, and he had notified prayer warriors of our situation and the need for prayer. He also contacted a local minister. We were praying as hard as we could that it be God's will to heal our husband and dad. I kept asking Jesus to put his healing hands upon my precious husband. We needed a miracle—a big one.

The girls and I also spent some time in the trauma center family waiting room, which was a huge room filled with recliner-type chairs, allowing you to spend the long hours stretched out as comfortably as possible and to sleep if you could. I couldn't sleep. I don't think the girls could, either. The room was usually packed with families waiting as we were, preventing us from even finding chairs by each other. Many nice people were there, but I really had no interest in meeting strangers right then.

Honestly, I focused so much on their dad, I know I had moments that I was not thinking about their comfort. I could not find a position that felt the least bit comfortable but I just thought about Steve held hostage in that cage holding his head. I had quit wearing the arm sling because I did not want Steve seeing it and worrying about me, and because it pulled on my neck, stirring up old neck injuries. No one was feeling great, and Terri had her five-year-old daughter, Laurel, with her to keep occupied for the dragging hours of each day. I don't know how we would have handled a less well-behaved child. She hung in there no matter what we were doing or where we had to do it.

I can only imagine how boring the status meetings were and how scary this all was for her. She had so many firsthand encounters of the worst kind in hospitals. Laurel was born with TAR syndrome. Put simply, she was born without radius bones in her forearms and her body failed to adequately produce platelets so vital to live. Every bump or fall resulted in emergency visits to have platelet transfusions. She had been through some serious surgeries in her short life and was now being scheduled for a bone marrow transplant, her only hope for survival. She had had so many transfusions that she needed the transplant before her body started rejecting transfusions.

There is nothing like having multiple crises at once. I worried about Terri as we dealt with this new crisis, but she and her sister were the arms that held me. I don't know what I would have done without them. Besides the moral support, Steve and I leaned on our girls to balance some of our reasoning on many topics. They were both smart and had good heads on their shoulders. Saying we were proud of them would be an understatement. We trusted their judgment. I fully trusted them with this unreal state of things.

My mind wandered frequently, replaying our life together, especially the early days. I found it hard to sleep at night because I couldn't stop praying and remembering how special Steve had always been to me. Tough as it was to get through the day, the night was torture, trying to sleep. I just wanted to escape as much as anything. Reality was a nasty dream and I kept wanting to just wake up from it, but it wouldn't go away. I tried to recall happier days, thinking about that cute guy I married.

2

Puppy Love

*S*teve and I became sweethearts when he was nine-teen and I was just seventeen. Other than sometimes outrageous family dramas, our lives were peaceful and filled with the normal struggles of balancing careers and raising children. In spite of the stresses we faced, we managed to work through the peaks and valleys of life and remain partners and lovers. Having worked hard to complete our educations and build satisfying careers, we both retired young enough to look forward to enjoying many years, driving the roads of the magnificent United States and reveling in Corvette car-avan trips. Steve loved his Corvette, and we loved the travel and people we encountered through his passion for it. No one could predict how soon—how abruptly—a trip to join one of those Corvette caravan events would change our lives. How could I walk away with a sprained shoulder, and Steve be so crumpled when I was sitting right next to him?

I met Steve while in high school and married him after a year of college. Being two years older, he had completed a year of college and joined the Air Force as his draft number fast approached, also giving him a means to leave home. In those days, the military was not an option, and there were no education waivers. My dad was transferred to Vandenberg AFB in California at the end of my junior year, and Steve was stationed there a month later as his first assignment out of basic training.

Leaving a high school of about 500 to enroll in a huge high school with a senior class of 550 left me unable to cheerlead or join some of the clubs I formerly enjoyed. Living on base had limitations, too, but I met a neighbor girl, also a senior, who worked at the dining hall. Since I had been told that I needed to work if I wanted a class ring, yearbook, special clothes, or other teen desires like records, the logical conclusion for me was to get a job. I had babysat since I was twelve, but that didn't pay consistently or as well as a real job.

I will not say I enjoyed it because I didn't! I bussed tables, did dishes, and served on the food line. Having been told how awful GIs are my whole life, I had no desire to know any of those guys coming through the line. Steve ate at the base dining hall where I worked. (You may note how hypocritical this upbringing was to dislike military men, considering my dad and brother were both military men! But my dad had been a training instructor at Lakeland AFB and had seen some pretty wild guys!)

Steve soon came through the line where I was serving and started talking to me. I was pretty cold! After all, he was one of "them." He was persistent and kept trying to get me to talk to him and asked me several times if I wanted to go to the base movie with him. I found him very cute and was quite attracted to him but refused to acknowledge him for a couple of months. Admittedly, ignoring him was difficult. He had started weight training while playing football in high school and was built! He was tall and had nice dark hair, a great physique, a great smile, gorgeous blue eyes, and was just manly, especially in that uniform! (I said I was cold, not blind.)

Then one day my friend asked me to go with her to the movie on base so she could meet this military guy. Her dad was opposed to her dating GIs, much like my dad, so she needed me to help her execute a date. Steve had continued asking me out, and I really had become smitten with him, so I told him I would meet him at the movie on base when I went with her. This was a big step for me, even if I did live only three blocks away. So, my friend picked me up, and we made the long journey around the corner. Steve was parked in the lot at the movie just as he said he would be. I had swirling butterflies in my stomach just anticipating seeing him. I really felt awkward and undeserving of his attention.

I got into his Volkswagen Bug, and we sat and talked until my friend emerged after the movie. That couple of hours passed like it was a few minutes. We talked about so many things and discovered so many parallels in our thinking, our desires for life, and feelings we had worked to suppress. We found joy in being able to laugh together. Steve was interested in my trust issues resulting from moving so frequently with my dad's Air Force career, especially since he was in his first summer in the Air Force. He shared how he had moved every year of high school when his parents divorced, after he grew up in the same house until his early teens. We both had learned social skills to appear more outgoing than we were and guarded against letting people get close.

He shared some of the hardships of working for his stepdad and mother, although he glossed over their alcoholism issues. I had friends with divorced parents, but I had never heard some of the things that Steve had to share about going back to court and restricting children from seeing their dad. It was beyond anything I would have expected to read in a novel, filled with cruel emotional and some physical abuse and such hatred. He had not been allowed to see his dad following his parent's divorce years earlier. He was expected to work without pay in various businesses his mother and stepdad started. He also became the housekeeper, which he hated and resented. Before the divorce, they had a live-in housekeeper and cook so the house was always well kept, but his mom did none of it. He was also frequently given responsibility for his younger brother, probably the only thing he didn't resent, even with usual brotherly annoyance.

As some reimbursement for years of working without pay, he had been given a car—a fun and stylish old Ford convertible. He also had bought some new clothes before starting college. When he left for basic training, he only took a change of clothes because he was issued what the Air Force wanted him to wear. After basic training, he visited his mother and stepdad before going to his first assignment, expecting to get his car and clothes. Wrong.

When Steve went home he discovered that in the six weeks he was gone, his mother had sold his car (his payment for years of free labor) and had given his clothes away! What! Incredible, I thought. As he shared that with me, he seemed to take it into his stride as though it was just how things were done. I told him I would be so angry. He just responded that his mother had problems, and he didn't need any of it, but he would never go back. He wanted nothing from anyone. He just wanted to be left alone.

They had loaned him the Volkswagen so he would have a car, expecting him to use it to drive home. He planned to go home as infrequently as he possibly could. Clearly, he felt betrayed by his family and could not stand the constant chaos and uncertainty. You were only as good as what they needed from you. He never wanted to go back, but at the same time, Steve was a very loyal person who still cared about his family in spite of hating to be around them. While this all sounded like an incredible story to me, it barely scratched the surface of their reality. I didn't question him because I could not imagine such a life, and I did not know where to begin. The pressure on him might have been less had he not been stationed so close to home.

Steve and I starting spending as much time as we could together. He was eating at our house every night, after eating at the dining hall! I admit to taking the sly approach of my friend who I helped meet her guy at the movie. Because Steve was taking a night course, I told my folks he was a college student! I know, I lied—by omission of total disclosure. I always got caught, so I assumed my time would come.

As a new airman without money we really couldn't afford to go to movies and out to eat, so our dating was mostly eating dinner with my parents and watching TV with them at our house. If we did go to the movies or to a drive-through food place, Steve bought one coke with two straws for us to share. Funny, we never got over that habit. He always preferred to share my drink than to have his own, right up to the last night we shared together!

Spending so much time around my folks, he grew on them, and they gradually learned to love him. With my brother stationed away from home in the Coast Guard, and Steve estranged from his dad, a mutual respect began to form between my dad and Steve in a very short time. I say respect because that did not mean my dad was gushing friendly to him. He was friendly to Steve but in a military superior way. My folks appreciated how polite and clean-cut he was. (Of course, I could not imagine bringing home a hippie!) I had not dated many guys and certainly never had boys at our house, so I think my folks liked us dating at home. Steve fit in. He was easy to be around.

Unfortunately, before I could fess up, my dad saw Steve in uniform one day and promptly came home to confront me with his shocking news. I knew it couldn't last forever. Fortunately, he liked Steve so much that he was already pretty well part of our family. And since Steve had been separated from his own dad, his bond with my dad became unusually strong as soon as we married. This seemed like the perfect relationship and joining of families to me because I could see how well my family accepted Steve. He even got along with my brother, and they seemed to genuinely like each other. I admit to thinking perhaps fairy tales were possible, or at least the happily ever after, but my mother made sure to keep me straight by jokingly labeling our relationship as "puppy love." Comments like that made me long to be with Steve away from the aggravation. I knew she did not mean it as an endearing label.

3

Holding On

*M*y thoughts were interrupted as visiting hour approached, and we needed to get to the hospital. No calls overnight meant that Steve was holding on or at least nothing had gotten worse. I went to see Steve first with Michele. I didn't know how to comfort him because he couldn't feel anything below his chin, and I could not deal with holding his ballooned up hand. Besides, he was in such a prone position with the erector set of the halo holding his head and neck in place. His face was untouched in spite of the massive scalp injuries. Michele said, "Mom, he can feel on his face if you want to touch there."

I started running my fingers around his face lightly massaging his temples where I could. The relaxation showed in his eyes as I did that. He could look at us although his eyes looked rather flat. He was unable to speak with the ventilator in his throat breathing for him. His body had already started to shut down functions from the spinal cord injury. Machines and medication were totally keeping him alive. Even though I realized that on some level, I couldn't think about not giving him every chance to recover. I was actively searching for remedies to care for a quadriplegic. I didn't care what I would have to do. This was the love of my life. I had to make it work.

Then Michele showed me I could reach over the apparatus and kiss his cheek. I leaned up to do that and just instinctively my lips met his and he puckered his lips ever so slightly to meet mine. He was responding. He opened his eyes and looked at us. I wondered what he was thinking. How I wanted him to speak. But since he couldn't, I just kept telling him that I loved him so much and that I was okay, the girls were there, and friends in Tyler were praying for him. I told him the roll bar he added must have saved us, which earned a weak little grin. I had complained about how close my seat was with it—one of those little inside jokes we shared. He seemed to acknowledge with his eyes. After a while, I left Michele with him and let Terri take my place beside him. Michele would come out shortly and let me join Terri. We spent many hours there on Saturday.

Ken, Terri's husband, had decided to get a flight and brought their older daughter, Darby, so he could see Steve. Steve and Ken always liked each other, and we lived next door so they knew each other pretty well. Since Laurel was with Terri, I think Ken bringing Darby, even for that quick visit, gave Terri a slight break. Laurel had been our main focus since her birth. She was a little trouper as we spent so many hours in the hospital—a tough place to hang out. Her cheery, sweet personality won the hearts of everyone we talked to and helped to keep us more level.

We had meetings with the medical team every day and sometimes more as Steve's condition was monitored and treated. Our meeting that Saturday made it pretty clear that the trauma doctor saw no glimmer of hope for recovery with Steve's age and the Parkinson's. We were all feeling deflated when Ken showed up, surprising us with his impromptu visit. As if Terri didn't have enough stress, Ken confessed he had left in such a hurry that he left their toy poodle out in the back yard! It was August in Texas and Barbie was a 100 percent pampered inside dog. When he remembered she was out, he had called his best friend to go retrieve the dog from the yard, but she was nowhere to be found! Panic set in. His friend put out fliers about the lost dog and searched the neighborhood to no avail. What a weekend!

Upon returning home, Ken discovered Barbie had decided they weren't letting her back into her house so she dug under our connecting fence and helped herself through the doggie door to our back porch. She was found sitting on the sofa in our enclosed patio. Our dog was at the vet for boarding because we were on our trip. Unfortunately, that meant there was no food or water sitting out for Barbie, but Ken was only gone a day so she was fine. We were all relieved they had found her, and she was surely happy to get to go home. I was glad Ken was able to come for Terri, as much as for Steve and me. The gesture was comforting, especially since they had quite a load on their shoulders already with the pending bone marrow transplant coming.

Michele and Jonathan had debated having her family come from Syracuse. They wanted to come, but we decided together that it was not the best plan for anyone. I knew they were there for us in spirit, and no doubt Steve knew Michele was there and that her family knew and cared about him. We had visited them in Syracuse just a month earlier. How glad I was that we were able to make that trip. It was one of our best times. Steve had especially treasured the time we spent with our two grandsons, Nick and Ben, and granddaughter, Maddy. Living so far away, we have not seen them as often as we would like.

I believed it better for them to remember him as his happy, kind, grandpa self who was totally mobile, instead of seeing him like this. The younger ones probably could not see him anyway, and I think the sight of him was very difficult. Besides, we had so little time with him, especially with only two visitors allowed at once. We spent so much time sitting around waiting.

We were all exhausted, as you might imagine. I felt so helpless except for the ability to talk to the Lord, which I did a lot. I found myself reflecting on how grateful I was for our life and, yes, praying that it be God's will, to please save Steve. I knew so many people were praying for us, many I did not even know. And so many people were so supportive, leaving messages and some stopping by. Gary came from Bowling Green to see Steve. What true, caring friends we found at the Corvette Museum. The doctors and nurses were professional but also warm and compassionate. The trauma doctor was probably more about business, but the nurses made up for his cooler bedside manner.

The girls were trying to keep Laurel entertained, and I was trying to stay calm. My nature is usually such, but this was pretty startling. I wept at times partly from the stress of it all and partly from sheer exhaustion. I felt oddly at peace at the same time I felt totally out of control. It was out of my hands. Only God could deal with this through the trained medical hands or some huge miracle, and I knew it. I did fall victim to some comments inferring God can save anyone if you pray hard enough. I tried not to fall under any false promise that I could control the outcome by praying hard enough. I believe we ask for God to save us, but I allow for His plan to supersede mine. I believe I can pray, and God will always answer, but He sometimes answers, "No."

I started remembering how I had experienced such an answer years earlier. I applied for a promotion that I badly wanted. My plan was to move to Texas from Florida for the promotion and to allow us to live closer to my dad and Steve's dad, both ailing at the time. I prayed for it diligently. The answer came back, "No." I was one of the final two, but the other guy was selected. I am ashamed to say that I was not only disappointed but I felt almost betrayed that I had prayed and did not get the job. I suppose I sulked a bit for the next few months. Then, without warning, I was called to interview for a new position in a new organization in Texas I had not even been aware of. I was hired for this position. Unbelievable!

The position that was given to the other guy wound up being moved to Connecticut, far away from Texas, and that position became part of the new organization I just acquired, reporting to me! God must have quite a sense of humor, and I imagined him laughing loudly at my selfish prayer tactics. I knew for sure then that it was totally true that God's plan was much better than mine. I needed to back off and stop being so demanding. God had plans for me that I could not even imagine, much better than what I tried to reach for. So, I knew I had to somehow trust God that if Steve was to be saved, my prayers needed to align with God's will. It had to do with what God knew to be best and how my obedience and prayer fit into that plan. I prayed for Him to help us through this, to make me able to support whatever needs Steve had, to provide the doctors with the wisdom to care for him, and for God to provide a miracle if it be His will. I knew it was beyond my hands. I do believe in prayer, and I do believe in miracles, but I don't know how it all comes together. God is so much bigger than life itself.

For I know the plans I have for you," declares the Lord, "plans to prosper you and not to harm you, plans to give you hope and a future. (Jeremiah 29:11)

My mind wandered to thoughts of family. Steve's mother and father were both deceased, and so were mine. I had talked to my brother and Steve's stepmom, Jackie. She was as dev-astated by it all, as were we. Who could imagine this? The whole thing seemed like a sleep-walking nightmare. We were up and walking but could not believe this was happening. I was glad I didn't have Steve's mother to deal with. I prayed praises for that.

We had been close to his dad and Jackie since Steve had reached out to his dad many years earlier, after Steve observed how his mother treated me and her irrational demands on him. I was so glad he, his dad, and stepmother had great times together and a special closeness before Steve's dad died. Jackie said she would let Steve's brother know what was going on. We never heard from him, but that was expected. I wished I could have told Steve that his brother was on the phone or something, but I doubt he even gave that a thought with how that part of the family had been. He only heard from his brother when he wanted Steve to do something or give something to their mother, and since she had died, Steve didn't hear from his brother.

During our first visit with his dad and Jackie, Steve and I had tried to help his then teenage brother escape the insanity and give him a chance with their dad. Steve wanted to help his brother as no one had done for him. In spite of our efforts to give him an opportunity for a better life, sadly, his brother wound up back with their mother after a short time. Steve felt helpless to fix any of the hateful strains of decades, and he did not want to be part of relationships full of grudges and demanding expectations. He felt guilty that his mother had dragged me into the fray because their family issues started before he knew me and had nothing to do with me. He did not want our family in any way brought into the greedy and spiteful relationships his mother had instituted. I couldn't help but think about how that family was.

4

Naïve Love

*H*ow naïve that I thought I could ever be accepted by Steve's mother and therefore his siblings. I was young and innocent, after all. I expected to have some measure of acceptance when I met his mom—I was wrong. I actually only saw her twice before we were married. Unknown to me, immediately upon learning we were dating, she had started criticizing me and trying to get Steve to stop seeing me. I was a senior in high school and then started college at a community college, so weekends were the only real time we had together, and he did not want to go home. Steve had given seeing me as a reason for not going home, but really he just didn't want to go home whether he was dating me or not.

He had left his family and never wanted any part of that lifestyle again. He felt constantly betrayed and unsafe around them. He hated that his brother was still there but felt helpless about that situation. Survival mode was his driving force. He tried to remain civil while avoiding contact. He wanted to pretend that he had a "normal" family, so he failed to share the dysfunctional facets of life in that environment. I suppose many of us find it hard to admit that marriage includes the whole family, not just the spouse. Escape was his only remedy. He was realistic enough to recognize he could not fix it. His mother would try anything to sabotage our relationship. She went so far as to set him up with a girl she knew to be very "fast" when he did go home one weekend. We had not been intimate, and he told me that he had no desire to be with that girl or any other. He said he knew we were going to get married. I loved him for that. He felt safe enough with me that he could even tell me about a girl set up to seduce him. I admit my thoughts about his mother left me puzzled. Was this woman as bad as she sounded? She certainly had peculiar methods for parenting.

I later learned that she kept telling him that I was just a military brat, and he was the son of a dentist, so I was trying to trap him for that reason, implying it was his money I was after. I always thought that sounded somehow obscene and very strange, considering how I put him off and he chased me. The truth was that her control over him failed, and she could not handle that. She had always forbidden him to have contact with his dad, even returning the gifts he sent him, still unopened. She also told him his dad never paid child support, but we discovered in truth, his dad had sent gifts for every occasion and consistently paid child support the whole time.

Steve's sister received her support directly but never told the boys about it so she skated through college fully funded with a car and a luxurious wardrobe financed by her dad. In fact, when we planned our wedding, we were not allowed to send an announcement to his dad and certainly not an invitation. I recall the day we showed his mom and sister the lists we had made, and they both started bashing his dad and telling me why we absolutely could not tell that awful man. He had been included in his sister's wedding, so it was odd to us that she and his mother protested so much. It seems that his dad could not be told because, even though Steve had been in the Air Force for two years, they were telling his dad that he needed to keep paying child support because Steve was in school.

Yes, the reason why Steve was not allowed to see his dad became clear. If Steve married and his dad found out, Steve's mom's income would shrink. She didn't care about losing Steve; she cared about herself. She had taken his dad for all she could get and always wanted more. She didn't know me at all to determine like or dislike. It wasn't me she disliked; it was what I represented. His mother always had to blame someone for her unhappiness, and I was the new scapegoat.

It seemed her own children were always to blame for her problems when they were growing up. She had told Steve several times that her life was good until she had had kids. How hurtful. Steve had told me over the years how she blamed him if her day went poorly or if she was in a bad mood. I guess booze can have such an effect, and she was an undiagnosed bipolar personality. Steve's dad had tried to get professional help for her, but she refused to go. Unfortunately, bipolar personalities were not well understood or treated that long ago.

Steve was a brand-new airman right out of basic training, and he had just completed a year at a community college when I met him. Money was the least of his offerings at the time. He had not seen his "dentist" dad for years. Money certainly had nothing to do with my attraction and love for Steve. I don't know if he would have tried to complete college had the draft not been active, but I do know that he would have left home some way. As much as he tried to overlook the chaos, deception, and hateful ways, he knew in his heart that he had to protect me from that family. I did try to befriend his mom, although I only saw her once after we married.

Although she wouldn't allow Steve's dad to know about the wedding, she failed to show up herself at the last minute. His stepdad had been celebrating with my dad at our house after the rehearsal dinner and became rather "happy." Steve had taken him back to the hotel, and his mother told him she would not be at the wedding because he let his stepdad get drunk! He laughed it off, and his buddy drove him back to the barracks. The next morning his stepdad showed up with just his brother. His sister and her husband were staying at my folk's house. Steve was embarrassed but shrugged it off and told me not to worry. He was a quiet master at stuffing things like that. Of course, my family and I were totally puzzled at the very strange behavior.

We were transferred shortly after we married. I would write to his mother when I wrote to my parents and tell her what we were doing and how we were, and she would respond by sending a letter special delivery to Steve so he had to sign for it. She would call person-to-person so she only spoke to Steve. She told Steve that she only heard from me so she knew I was keeping things from him. He told her that he was not a letter writer, and that was why she only heard from me, but I would not be writing any longer. With that, all correspondence ended. A year later, she returned a gift unopened. Hmmm.

Because Steve had mentioned little things every so often about his dad, I knew it ate at him that he had not heard from him or been allowed to see his dad for so long—nine years! All he had heard was hate about him all those years and any mention of seeing him was met with scorn and threats. He had once told his mom he was going to see his dad, and she told him to come home because she reported him for stealing the car. Imagine. I guess she then told the authorities it was a mistake, so nothing was done to him, but Steve got her point. Nothing was beneath her. She was obsessed with controlling everything and everyone. Any mention of seeing his dad was met with threats of being disowned. Strange as it sounded, Steve still desired to be loved by his own mother. I've heard abused kids react that way.

Steve said every day had peaks and valleys, based on her moods. Nothing was ever her fault. She never apologized. This became important to understand as our years together hit times of peaks and valleys. I discovered that her behavior had seriously scarred his expectations of women. He was not aware how affected he had been by her illnesses. He was devastated by the impact her character had on their family. He could not tolerate any emotional demands. His coping mechanisms were stretched beyond full recovery. He shut down his emotions and held everything inside, putting on a happy exterior. His mother used illness, tears, and hysterical anger to control. Steve knew it made no sense, but he shrank into his shell every time she started screaming at him, usually for things he had nothing to do with. She was illogical, blaming, and irrational. She was a manic-depressive alcoholic.

How did their divorce happen? While cruising to Hawaii with his dad, who was trying to reconcile after eighteen years of a turbulent marriage, she decided to leave him for the bartender on the ship! Yes, a family was taken down by boredom. She admitted it to Steve the last time he spoke to her when she was dying. She had no remorse or regrets. The children became pawns in one of the nastiest divorces imaginable because she was bored. His dad believed giving her everything instead of fighting her because of her adultery would make it easier on the kids. In 1959, women were believed to be the better single parent, and he wanted the children spared the evil truth of her cheating. He must have hoped her character would be more civil with the kids than it was with him.

Unfortunately for everyone, winning was not enough for his mother. She was never satisfied and would never give up trying to get more. Clearly, she was blind concerning any impact on the family. She felt *she* deserved to be happy, whatever that meant and whoever it hurt. All the greed and spoils were spilled on booze, and she died broke. It is a very sad story but even more sad is the collateral damage she left in her wake. When Steve learned of her death, he said he felt relief, not loss. He did go to her funeral and told me not to go with him. He felt obligated to family but had no respect for her. He did want to see his siblings and their children who attended, but he wanted to remain distant.

I thought how fortunate now that his mother was dead and that group was not contacting us. Nothing positive had ever come in communication with them. Some people just feel the need to start conflicts by drudging up old stuff, even when they don't know what they are talking about. They like to fight. They only called us to stir up trouble or to ask for something—usually money. I had never known people who dwelled on the negative and used people like they did. Steve and I had always shielded our girls from that dysfunction. I was grateful for that. Steve wanted no part of carrying on the grudges and hatefulness. He just wanted to be left alone. We had tried to help his brother all those years ago, being instrumental is getting him out of that environment with the opportunity to live with his dad. I always thought how caring Steve was to do that, considering no one ever tried to help him like that, and the fact that we could have ignored his brother, but Steve and his dad wanted to help. In fact, our first meeting with Steve's dad was filled with energy to find out about his brother and insisting Steve should go visit his mother and siblings! What a contrast to how negative his mother had always been. Steve and I were both eager to help any way we could. Family was important to us.

As our relationship strengthened with Steve's dad and stepmom, Jackie, we decided to invite them to our second renewal of vows. We renewed our vows on our 10th, 25th, and 35th anniversaries. Steve really liked doing that. (Steve had asked me to again renew them before our 44th, but I regrettably said we should wait until our 45th!) For our 25th anniversary, we wanted Steve's dad to be there since he was not at our wedding. He and Jackie joined us in Las Vegas where we said our vows in a lovely ceremony at one of the little chapels on the strip. We had the limo and the whole flowery thing! We spent a few days there before going to Hawaii for two weeks.

How special to recall Steve's loving family being with us that wonderful day. We had a spectacular two weeks, one week on Oahu and one week on a cruise ship visiting all the islands. What fun days those were to remember!

As I thought about family, it again occurred to me that my parents were both gone, and Steve's parents were gone. I had Jackie, who I was close to, and my girls. My brother had been scarce since he left home as a teen to join the Coast Guard. We did not communicate regularly. It was Steve that I relied upon. He was the only long-term friend I had because of moving so much. Jackie was next. I had a few friends from when I worked and from church but we were still new to Texas. It was Steve I needed to talk to, and I couldn't. We could complete each other's sentences; we knew each other so well. Feeling alone is putting it mildly. My daughters were there for me, but they were leaning on their husbands, their closest friends—just what I really wished I could do.

I dreaded going to the meeting with the trauma team that would start the next morning. I was so exhausted, and yet I was anxious to find out what was happening with Steve. I wanted to see him. The sun was peeking through the curtain before I knew it. The room was quiet as we took turns taking our showers. I was glad we shared a room. I was not staying alone, at least.

5

Decision Time

We got to see Steve on Sunday during the early visiting time before the meeting with the trauma team. I looked at him with double vision. I could see the distorted body and all the apparatus keeping him alive. But, I also could see the man behind those eyes that still made my heart skip a beat. It was still my Steve in there. I so wanted him to miraculously show them that God had just put a hand on him and he was healed. Oh, how I prayed that would happen. But, it wasn't happening. The best we could do was make sure he was as comfortable as possible.

In talking to the nurse about Steve and some of his happiest moments, I remembered how he loved to watch *Jay Leno's Garage*, a show about his fabulous collection of all kinds of special automobiles and motorcycles. Steve would watch that glued to the screen. How he loved cars. He said when he was too small to reach the top of his dad's car, he would put a step stool in the drive so he could reach the roof to wash it. His stress reliever was fooling with a car or reading about them or seeing shows about them. He had become an expert about cars over the years and found driving to be his favorite relaxation. As mentioned earlier, the love of

Corvettes in particular started when he was learning to drive. He first drove on the Los Angeles freeways in, you guessed it, a Corvette. How he loved that American dream car.

Knowing how much he enjoyed Jay Leno, the girls and I inquired with the nurse about bringing in a laptop and letting him listen through earbuds. She thought it was a great idea if it was something he would enjoy. The girls set it up, and the minute he heard Jay Leno's voice and heard him talking about a car and could see a glimpse of it on the laptop his face softened and his eyes closed with a relaxed look about them. His face began to have a happy look to it even without a real smile. The nurse was pleasantly surprised with the noticeable change that came over him. He seemed somewhat soothed— anyway, as much as a person imprisoned in a halo without the ability to move or feel his own body might feel.

Feeling happy at the sight of Steve experiencing some tiny element of pleasure, I was promptly shaken back to reality when we had our scheduled trauma team meeting. Charts were discussed with us, with me mostly looking to the girls to understand levels of seriousness, especially Michele. Being a doctor, she certainly took in much more and could place more objectivity on the facts, in spite of her own emotional balancing act.

The news was not good. Steve was not improving. And, let's say it again so no one forgets—he was sixty-five and had Parkinson's. He had a complete spinal cord injury and was a quadriplegic. Nothing could change that. He would not be able to survive as Steve Reeves did. No matter how good the care or equipment, he was not going to be able to function. I heard it. I knew it was true. But my heart could not accept it. Even my brain fought to rationalize what I heard. Much silence followed. We were offered time to absorb what we heard and consider the living will. Living will? Why is it called that? It is a will about dying. I knew Steve would not want to suffer any longer than necessary, but how do you tell anyone to shut off the machines and medicine keeping your husband alive? I could not help but feel like I was being asked to kill him, even though I knew it was not exactly like that—not exactly.

Later that day the trauma doctor spoke to us again. I knew we had to decide about turning off the life support. He told us he wanted us to have Steve moved to Hospice and shut it all down there! What? Why would I move Steve to a new place and go through such trauma as moving him anywhere? Wasn't he traumatized enough as it was? I felt sick. I was having a hard time taking in where we were, but this new suggestion was cruel and insensitive. I know Hospice is kind and gentle and meant to help people in their last moments, but why would we undo what he had here to hook him up some-place else to undo it all again—and move him? Good grief! This was my husband, not a piece of furniture.

Steve had compassionate nurses who had obviously gained his trust and comfort with them. We were even able to have some lighter moments with them as one of them started a thing about how cute his feet were. They were, but she had no idea how funny that was because Steve did not like feet. He did not want anyone putting their feet on him or their socks or shoes. Feet had long been a running joke around our house. You could see a little color come into his cheeks as we laughed around him talking about how they liked his feet. I know he had to be laughing inside, even though he could not outwardly show it. I could almost hear his laugh in my head. No way did I want to leave care givers that he had clearly come to like in these short, awful two days.

I especially was protective of this because he had been so healthy. He had been in the hospital for the first time the previous December when he had an intestinal attack resulting from the Parkinson's. He *hated* being in the hospital even though he was miserable enough to agree to go to emergency that time. He especially hated it because, like this time, we were not home. We had just spent a week with our family at Disney World and were ready to drive home. Oh my. I just thought about how curious it was that his two hospital stays were out of state—very inconvenient. Actually, I do know that being hospitalized is inconvenient wherever you may be. None of us look forward to such visits.

Michele knew I was having a hard time with the Hospice suggestion, so she investigated for us and discovered that the hospital had a physician that specialized in end-of-life situations. We all agreed we did not want him moved. The doctor set a time to meet with us, inviting us to a more casual setting than the cold, clinical meeting room.

She clearly understood our concerns with moving Steve and assured us that the trauma center staff could more easily allow a respectful, compassionate, and peaceful end without moving him. She seemed to appreciate the tough situation for medical staff who saw the results of catastrophic events every day and the doctor less willing to remove life support. She said they usually were faced with people dying in spite of their efforts without the gut-wrenching task of withdrawing life support. I heard the explanation, but I could not understand why the burden would then be placed so heavily on the shoulders of family ill-equipped to deal with this impossible emotional decision.

I told her we could not compound the decision by jockeying Steve around with a move and all new people! The doctor looked into my eyes and said, "I can see that you are feeling guilty because you survived with a sprained shoulder." I started to cry. I just could not contain it any longer. Everything I had been trying to contain flooded out. She had hit the button square on. Yes, I did feel like I should be dead or at least in a bed beside Steve. Yet, here I was walking and talking. I was banged up and hurt, but I was fine. I don't believe in asking "why?" because I believe that will not be known until we are in Heaven. I believe there is a plan for the life of each of us, and somehow this was ours. But I did not like our plan with what I could see of it at that moment!

After spending some time with us talking through our feelings and appreciating them, we knew we had to decide. Although Steve could not communicate his wishes in his condition, we all knew exactly how he felt about such situations. We had both agreed that should we be faced with a life-support situation like this, we would honor the decision not to be sustained that way. We both had living wills. I knew I would not want to live that way, and it was inevitable that more serious problems would ensue the longer he was left in this condition.

Without medication, his heart rate dropped to critical levels, he could not breathe on his own, and fluid continued to swell his paralyzed body. No, I did not want to feel that I chose the hour he would be pronounced dead, but that was precisely the task at hand and that was what I would have to do. The nurses would get him cleaned up and start a process of sedating him so he was completely comfortable, allowing him to slip into a peaceful forever sleep when the time to turn off support was scheduled. The doctor suggested eleven o'clock the next morning, so we would be between visiting hours, allowing us to gather family and a minister around him and stay as long as we needed. So, it was scheduled. We were planning the end, the final chapter, *for* him *not with* him. Unbelievable! I did not make decisions without him. Rationalizing that he had decided by his instructions when we agreed to how we wanted such situations handled was of little comfort.

We stayed at the hospital spending every minute with Steve that we possibly could. We had added more entertainment for Steve by playing music from Foreigner that he liked. Again, he seemed to relax when he heard the music. The funny thing was how the nurses reacted. They loved it and said it made the whole place feel lighter. They played it out loud so they could hear it. I wished there was something else we could do. How do you comfort someone who is—I couldn't think about that word.

I leaned up to kiss his lips and kept stroking his face gently for as long as I could. He clearly liked that. He moved his lips as if to tell us he loved us when we kept telling him how we loved him. I also told him I knew how he loved Jesus and how much Jesus loved him. He acknowledged as best he could through his eyes. How I longed to think of anything to fix this! But my only comfort was to admit that everything was in God's hands. I so badly wanted to confer with Steve as I always had about everything. He was my very best friend. I had known him longer than anyone. We had always been there for each other.

This had been one of the longest days. As we returned to the hotel, I longed to sleep, but I just kept thinking about how Steve filled my life. A movie of our life kept progressing through my mind with such vivid pictures of our togetherness. I could almost feel his hand holding mine, the thing I loved the most about being with him. Something just made that gesture so sweet and caring. Oh, how I love that man! I kept thinking, "I can't lose him! I can't tell them to turn off his life!" He was my life.

My mind continued to wander through our love story, my favorite movie! Steve had said the morning of the accident, "I feel like I did when we first got together. I am so happy. I love you so much. I want to marry you again." I can only say his words meant so much to me. I kept thinking them over and over, holding on.

We had been married over forty-four years and together forty-six years. He wanted to get married again. The three times we had renewed vows, we both found it to be a refreshing and a fun way to reignite our life together. I loved how he liked that ceremony, that romantic promise of continued love, that covenant before God. As I kept playing that conversation over in my head, it made me drown in thoughts of our early days. We had gone through the daily grind years of raising a family and working hard at careers, paying bills, moving, running from school activity to school activity, surviving his family, fitting in our own education—but we had come back to regain the excitement of our early years. Life was good! We were happy. I loved *our* movie in my mind.

6

Enduring Love

*Y*oung as we were, we felt right away that we were just supposed to be together. We were in love and so compatible. We became inseparable. Both of us came from our own dysfunctional backgrounds and were convinced we could make a better life together and build a loving family. We had no fairytale fantasy. We had a strong attraction to each other, filled with a deep love and a desire to treat and be treated with respect. We really liked each other as friends and found trust in each other that neither of us had yet known. Although very different and on different scales, we both had mothers who only understood motivation through criticism and threats.

We spoke matter-of-factly about how life would be when we were married from the early weeks of our relationship. Yes, that was when I was still in high school. I suppose my mother had good reason to refer to our affections as "puppy love." I suppose dog love starts as puppy love and matures. I found that label for our relationship insulting, however. I always knew that Steve was the love of my life. Yes, mine was a short life at that point, but our love was very real to us. Our feelings deepened as we dated, and we grew closer and closer to each other. We felt safe together—something neither of us had experienced. Steve was respectful, not grabby. Besides, we sat in my parent's living room on most dates. This relationship was not just hormones, although there were those, too.

Many of my friends married as soon as they graduated from high school, so our plans did not seem that unrealistic to us in the early sixties. Besides, I was programmed to be a wife and mother. Any ambitions I might have had about getting a college education were put down as ridiculous—a total waste, knowing I was "just a girl" and my future would be as wife and mother. The expectation was so emphatic that I was directed to obtain certification for a civil service secretary by the end of my junior year. My mother was a secretary, so I was expected to follow that path and have a family. I was frequently reminded I was just a girl, and because my brother, a boy, did not go to college, I was silly to think such thoughts. The problem was my lack of motivation to be a secretary. I had no issue with women being secretaries if that was their choice of what they wanted to do. I simply did not want to do that. But I did as I was told, passing tests for typing and shorthand to receive certification.

Being a girl, I was not allowed to leave home until I was married. I believe my mom cared about me, but she had no understanding of my desire to go away to college. With that rule, I continued my education at a community college and, not being allowed to have a car, rode a school bus an hour each way every day. On days when I had only a class or two, I worked as my English teacher's secretary. (I guess my mom was right about having a useful skill!) The bus service was a high-school bus, so I went early each morning and returned late that evening. Acknowledging a poor attitude, I can best explain that situation as negative. I really wanted to go off to college, not feel I was merely extending high school. Although I always enjoyed learning, that situation felt restricting and demeaning. I don't apologize for being a teen and having some rebellious attitudes because I went along with the expectations in spite of my disappointment and lowered self-esteem.

During our courtship Steve and I bonded ever stronger as we both clung to the freedom we felt to be ourselves with each other. We accepted each other as we were. Nothing feels as free as feeling loved for being you. Isn't that how God loves us? I had not felt such love from another person, and Steve kept telling me he had never felt that way before. Everyone seemed to have conditions attached as if you had to earn love. Of course, we were physically attracted to each other (I thought he was a real hunk!), but we did not leap into a sexual relationship like movies of today. Our excitement was to spend time together, playing tennis or things like touch football. Yes, football.

We enjoyed watching football and routing for teams with my dad when he was around. Having been a cheerleader, I had appreciation for the game. Practicing touch football became a necessity when I played in a Powder Puff Game at the community college I was attending. Steve ran with me and showed me plays until I would drop from exhaustion. It was fun! How I loved his guy skills. I was in awe at how easily he seemed to move and roll and run barely breathing hard. How I wished I could do that. I was breathless, aching, and bruising. He was so strong and yet so gentle and sweet. What a combination. He really stole my heart.

Steve had mentioned how undemonstrative his parents were. Such insights into his family were so sad. He pledged to be demonstrative with our children. Clearly, showing love was something he not only wanted to feel but he wanted to learn to display. As I said, "puppy love" was how my mother coined our affection for each other. I can appreciate her concern as young as we were. But age is only one factor of maturity. Steve and I had grown up much more quickly than most people our age due to our unique circumstances. To her annoyance, I reminded my mother that she and my dad were only seventeen and nineteen when they married. I know my mom worried about us struggling as she and my dad had, but I couldn't see why she didn't understand how I felt. Besides, their marriage worked!

My world was molded by an overbearing mother doing her best to control uncontrollable life. My father was often gone, we moved frequently with the military, and my brother left immediately following high school. In fact, my brother left for the service the same day my dad flew to England, leaving my mother and me alone for nine months. I was starting seventh grade in Waco, Texas. We had moved from San Antonio six weeks before I finished sixth grade. My brother was allowed to stay with friends to graduate from high school so he was only with us in Waco a few months until he and my dad left that August. My brother is six years older than me, so he graduated from high school the same day I graduated from grade school that year.

Control monsters took over my mother that year. Her tool of choice was criticism. I truly believe my mother felt I was the only thing she could control through such times. Well, I was the only one around. I never doubted I was loved, but the strain of that relationship never improved after that year. The more she tried to control, the more resentment I felt. I can't say that I dreamed of getting out because I was only twelve, but I did know that I wanted to be independent and included in decisions someday.

Looking back on it as an adult and mother, I admit her need to control became more understandable. My mother grew up during the Great Depression, raised by a mother who was widowed quite young with five children. Being the youngest, my mother must have carried heavy memories of hardships in her life that unfortunately left her bitter, but she never shared any of that. I do know that she lost an older sister and her dad when she was a small girl. Her coping mechanisms had to have been fully tested. She likely did not talk about her younger days because the pain of them made her want to forget them. Realizing that, I could later appreciate that she and my dad, who was raised by his grandfather, must have experienced many of the very emotions and frustrations that Steve and I did. Many emotional parallels were evident in comparison.

By the last semester of seventh grade when I had turned thirteen, my parents decided that separation was not good, and my mom and I should join my dad in England. I was working to complete classes early so we could move. The principal interrupted my math class and asked for me to go with him. I thought it must be something about my finishing school early, but he took me to the hospital. My mother had been robbed at work at gunpoint and a telephone was used to fracture her skull. I found myself alone faced with trauma. My dad's voice played in my head telling me to be strong and responsible. He always said we could not control what happened to us, but we could control how we reacted. I had to act *mature*. That was the word. I grew up not understanding my mother but appreciating her. The robbery and her visible fear and vulnerability made me appreciate her more. But, our relationship did not change.

I was a normal teenager, although I was generally dutiful and went along without making waves. In spite of my cooperation, I could not please my mom, and my dad was usually unavailable. With my parents both working, I was a latchkey kid from early elementary school. I actually hated coming home by myself and being the first to open that front door. I would search closets and under beds to make sure no one was lurking in the house. I don't know if they ever thought of that. I wanted to be taken care of and be dependent. I hungered for unconditional love and a chance to be myself and pursue my own dreams, including an education my parents could not understand. I also wanted to be a kid and not feel so responsible for myself. They had completed high school, but in those times, college was not for everyone. The fact that they started a family in very difficult times and provided us with a comfortable life was quite an accomplishment—not that I recognized or appreciated that as a teen.

Steve had been dealing with much more than I could imagine in his family. He was a master of shoving his feelings and pain to some hidden place within him. He grew up feeling unable to please anyone, blamed for most problems, and feeling even his own mother didn't love him. His parents divorced when he was a young teenager after years of turmoil. His mother had taken off with another man who abruptly became his stepdad. His mother's explanation in her final days of life was simply, "I was bored." Really? Bored? An entire family was trashed because she was bored? Her treatment of her family was inexcusable. Steve was not allowed to communicate with his dad in any way once she left his dad, and he had no say in who he lived with. He didn't know his dad had tried to contact him unsuccessfully, and therefore, felt rejected by him, making it easy for him to consider his mother's lies.

The nightmare of living with alcoholics, complicated by a manic-depressive mother, left him desperate for freedom and a desire to achieve something. In addition to being the housekeeper, he had to wash and iron any clothes he wanted to wear. He was expected to take care of himself and do whatever was needed to keep the house running. He also worked in whatever business his mom and stepdad started, which changed every year. By his senior year, the business was a resort in northern California. Steve felt trapped in a family of hurricane waves with his mother's mood swings. Even having joined the service, his mother had tried to continue to influence him when she had moved to Southern California.

By the time Steve had two years in the Air Force, he was selected for a transfer to Omaha, Nebraska for a great assignment opportunity. We had gotten married and were eager to leave California behind us. Vietnam was in full swing, and we had lost friends to the war. Naturally, we had both feared that Steve would have to go, but our perceived blessing was this opportunity to start a new life together our way.

We were not only going to be together but we were going to be many states away from the negative influences of his family. We had been going to services at the Vandenberg AFB, California chapel and really liked the chaplain that married us. He led us through the pre-marriage counseling and expressed how strongly he felt we were meant to be together. At the wedding, he shared his pleasure in marrying two people who clearly displayed love for each other by the intensity with which we connected through our eyes while repeating our vows. He said, "This is one of the most sincere services of joining together under God that I have done." We certainly felt that way. This was our chance for our life together. It began with a military wedding—oh, those men in dress uniforms were so stunning. Steve wanted to do that because he did love the Air Force, and he wanted to honor my dad. Steve's buddies were all in dress blues, and my brother represented the Coast Guard well. Steve's stepdad served as best man in a tux.

We started our journey together with absolutely nothing but our mutual love, a willingness to work hard, and a desire to support each other. Admittedly, I thought at the time my support of his Air Force job was just a temporary thing as I worked as a secretary. I was clearly ready to leave the military life behind me, from my perspective as a dependent. I don't know if he would have volunteered if there wasn't a draft, but he ultimately found a home in the Air Force with stability he had lacked at home and wound up making it his career. When we had our daughters, I was a stay-at-home mom, and Steve loved our life of coming home to us, a clean house, and a hot meal—meat and potatoes, of course! I loved that time of our lives also.

The military gave him a home where he could excel through discipline and dedication, and he was a sincere patriot. He loved this country so much he had volunteered for Vietnam along with his buddies when he first joined the service. When he cross-trained as part of his reenlistment, he was faced with five sets of orders to Vietnam but was no longer eligible with his new career field. He had become a cartographer, responsible for working on targets for pilots and could only be stationed in the United States for security reasons. I was initially disappointed when he decided to reenlist. As it turned out, the military provided a good life in spite of the many sacrifices, mainly for him, but also for our daughters and me. At any rate, I vowed to be there through better or worse, so I was going to be there even if I thought it was better for him and worse for me at times.

I first learned of Steve's coping mechanisms after we were married. I chuckled inside remembering the first time I was upset and crying. I think his mom had sent him a note telling him to come home by himself, which really hurt my feelings! I was making spaghetti for dinner and telling him through my tears how much that tore into my feelings when I heard a loud, gurgle-sounding snore. What—listening to me put him to sleep? Yes, a trick he had learned from his dad in his youth—when the going gets tough, go to sleep! I was incensed. I shook him and told him he needed to wake up and listen to how upset I was! We laughed about it many times since then, but I was so upset then. The humor definitely escaped me at the time.

Steve grew up in a family that enjoyed financial wealth but lived in emotional poverty. His dad had become a wealthy dentist. I thought about how I had asked Steve after we married if it bothered him that he didn't live the "good life" anymore. I recall him saying without hesitation, "It was never mine. It was my dad's. I do have the 'good life' now." I respected his ability to leave all the hurt behind him, although I didn't realize until many years later how he hid his pain so deeply inside that it haunted him. We both wanted to raise a family and do well, but money was not important. A loving family was all that mattered. We totally agreed on that, and it served us well to allow us to let go of relationships that were hurtful. We were conservative, and if we didn't have money, we didn't buy stuff. If people did not want us in their lives, we weren't. Simple. I was a stay-at-home mom until our younger daughter started kindergarten. We had less money, so I made clothes and cooked from scratch. We lived independently and asked for nothing from anyone. We were probably our happiest when we had nothing. We always had each other. We appreciated having a family unit that loved each other. (Yes, we had loving daughters who fought with each other—lovingly!)

Although his parents divorced when he was a teen, the emotional damage had built from his childhood. As a small child, Steve became so upset when his mother had one of her meltdowns that he would become physically ill, throwing up. His life growing up is a story to itself, but it was his ability to overcome so much negativity that drew me closer to him year after year. It was tough enough having a bipolar mother, but to add alcohol was a real train wreck. His dad had been ill equipped to cope with his mother's irrational behavior, even though he tried desperately to keep the family together. She blamed him for everything and was a hysteric. The effects on the family were tragic, especially with such a vindictive mother.

Steve was the middle child in their family, caught in the mediator position but with the personality to hold the stance. Steve had developed an uncanny ability to compartmentalize parts of his life. As many children of alcoholics seem to camouflage themselves, he was a cheerful outgoing person away from home as though all was well. I knew him as an easy-going, rather quiet, kind young man who would shut down rather than allow himself to carry on any sort of feud or argument. He had a gift for letting go and not holding grudges. I don't know that it was really forgiveness, but he certainly seemed able to forget. (Like most women, I had the opposite trait. It was so hard for me to forget, even when I sincerely focused on forgiving.) Consequently, that skill eventually seemed to overflow from him to me, and we did not argue, although that is not to say we never got angry. The minister who married us commented that he expected us to have a good marriage based on seeing us in church together and our approach to the pre-marriage counseling. He predicted that accurately. We had a good marriage, basically growing up together and helping each other mesh old habits. (Note: I did not say perfect!) I learned to calm down and think more, and he learned (much later) to talk more and allow some feelings to surface.

Steve could not tolerate arguing and negativity. He would walk away if he heard people talking badly about another person. He clearly heard enough growing up. Not only was his mother hysterical much of the time and blamed him for her miserable life, but he felt his older sister had bullied him. He had a serious problem stuttering as a child that surely developed as a result of the constant chaos and taunting. He cared for his younger brother and tried to support him as much as a child can while living in survival mode, but by the time the draft was breathing down his neck, he was desperate to escape his captivity. He just wanted out! No hope for change existed as long as he lived at home. He felt like a pawn in a major battleground all the time. His only options were to shut down and leave when he could. Steve was scarred with an inability to cope with turmoil; he was only able to shut down and go to sleep.

His mother always needed someone to blame, and I was an easy target, so she lashed out at me, even though she did not know me. I suppose she had to convince herself that Steve would be loyal to her if it were not for me. The truth was that he dismissed her and his life around the hatefulness before he met me. I doubt I would have met him had she treated him differently. He chased me, not the other way around, as she always accused me of doing. He was also the one who adamantly protected our family from exposure to that negativity.

The minister had been a bit concerned about Steve's religious upbringing but was happy that we had been relying upon the church as we dated and developed our relationship. I had grown up going to nondenominational churches on military bases, usually with my brother once he started driving. Steve had a mother who was a nonpracticing Catholic and a father who was Mormon. Yes, he had very conflicting foundations. Steve, in fact, had attended a Catholic school at times while infrequently attending Mormon church on Sunday. At some point, he started sporadically attending an Episcopal church. He believed in Jesus but was confused about how the story fit together. I am sure the minister would have been more concerned had Steve shared the real story about his mother and the life he left behind him. I know that I might have been. As madly in love as I was, I don't think it would have changed my desire to marry, but I might have kept an eye out and not been so naïve going into it.

Happiness for Steve came from feeling some control. I knew him as one able to control his life, and it felt positive. I didn't feel he was trying to control me, but I recognized his need to feel in control. Things at home had been unpredictable and totally out of his control. The military provided a very predictable environment that gave him great comfort. Cause and effect were promised and given. He became comfortable with the ability to have some control over his life.

And he felt like he belonged right away. He was accepted, and he appreciated this black-and-white lifestyle.

My thoughts bounced around constantly. This movie in my mind had so many good stories, and we appreciated that God had blessed our lives so many times. We had a wonderful family, a wonderful life, just like we wanted. We had good careers and lived a great life together. We had overcome difficulties and remained a strong team. We were blessed with two daughters who remained fairly close. How special it had been for us to even have them both living at home for some of their college years. We loved that!

I kept thinking how young Steve was at sixty-five and what a great time in our life we were having. (I know that it is all relative. I used to think my parents were "gonners" when they were in their sixties. I remember my mother turning forty, and I thought she was way past middle age. How quickly perspectives change.) I knew I had to get some sleep and quit playing our life's movie in my head, but the thought of the current reality was just too much to bear. How could I deal with life without Steve?

I loved this man so dearly. I know that we are not the only love story or the only proud parents or the only people that have overcome backgrounds with struggles and hardships. But, this is the only life I have known. This is the only man I shared my life with—married forty-four years! So many years together sounds very long, but living it seemed so short. How strange how our minds can make time seem so skewed. I remember the day we married, the day each of our girls were born, the day we retired—all of it seems to be in such a short time span, and yet it had been over all those many years. I know God knows all, but I could not stop telling him over and over how grateful I was for my gifted life with Steve and asking for it to continue as I pondered what we would face in the morning.

7

Until Death Do Us Part

By the time we arrived at the hospital on Monday, people and papers were waiting for us. Why does everything take so many papers? My stomach was in knots, my heart was racing, and my mind was a blur. We met with the doctor to confirm the plan. We would be able to stay with Steve as long as we wanted, all together. The two-person rule did not apply. Herb had helped us from Tampa to find a local minister, who was there to pray for Steve and us. We could all gather around the bed with curtains drawn all around us, so we were in our own space within that huge room of beds and miracle machines.

I don't remember everything clearly, but I cherished a little more time with Steve. I just looked at Steve and touched his face. I could not see that he realized we were there, but somehow I knew he did. I felt like God had answered our prayers, responding that He wanted Steve now. I do recall flashback thoughts of a month earlier that I found oddly comforting.

At a special July 4th celebration at our church, Vietnam veterans were honored. Steve had gone up for the prayer time for them. The guest speaker was a veteran of that war who had faced death and been saved miraculously. His message was about how when facing death, he prayed only to be saved. He did not mean he was asking for his life to be saved. He had been a Christian that walked away from his belief and had not been behaving as he should have been for many years. He was praying for Jesus to allow him to be saved—to accept Jesus before he died. All of a sudden an unscheduled helicopter came from nowhere and saved him. His entire unit had been killed, and he was so badly injured they thought he was dead. His body was placed in the helicopter among other body bags, but he was alive and saved. He spoke about how we all need to know that we could die at any moment. We could be killed on the way home that night. We never know when our time will come, but we do know that we have the opportunity to be saved and to recommit. He invited people to go forward and commit or recommit.

Steve had walked up to the front again and recommitted his love and belief in Christ. We had talked about that extensively. Steve was so moved by that story and how that man had been changed by his horrific but uplifting experience. Steve and I had joined the church years earlier and had been baptized together as a profession of faith, but Steve felt pulled to reconfirm that day. I was in the choir watching him, moved to tears, realizing how important it was to him. As we waited for the final moments to allow him the peace of his final human journey, I thought how special it was that we had been a part of a church with sincere hearts for the Lord. Our faith and relations with Jesus had become life for us. I felt strongly that Steve would be going to Heaven. I wished he could tell me what it was like.

Then the time came! We were all together around Steve's bed. The minister prayed as we held hands around Steve. I was so glad our girls were there, although I only saw Steve. I tried to hold on to the vision of him laughing or teasing me or giving me one of his looks. But, he didn't move. He didn't look.

His eyes were closed, and he was peaceful. The heart medicine had been stopped, and then the respirator was stopped. I was feeling sad, anxious, scared, guilty, and many other indescribable things, watching for him to stop breathing. After a few minutes, I looked and panicked as I saw his chest still indicating breaths being taken. Wait! He was breathing on his own! I looked at my daughter, Michele, the doctor. The look on her face made me panic worse because she looked in shock.

I looked at the nurse and said, "He is breathing on his own!" I was thinking, "What have I done? He could have made it! Why did we do this? We should have waited!" The nurse calmly said, "This is not unusual. Some air is still in the body, but he cannot breathe without the machine." Michele said she was surprised because she cares for premature babies that are so tiny they do not keep breathing like that. The minutes until Steve's vital signs flatlined seemed endless, although it was a matter of minutes. I was shaken but felt a quiet, peaceful calm.

The nurse commented how calm I was. What was I supposed to do? I was numb, and there was nothing I could do. This was so out of my hands that hysteria wouldn't help, I thought. I was drained emotionally. Besides, my dad had taught me over and over that I could not change life or things that happened, but I could learn to deal with them. Although I did not know how to deal with this, I knew I had to somehow accept God's plan, like it or not. I did not like it, but I was in the midst of it.

Just as I was convincing myself we needed to leave and somehow finish any tasks left, a call came, asking me to donate Steve's organs. We had agreed to do that on our driver licenses, so as difficult as it was, I asked Michele to talk to them for me. I could not talk. I could not believe they would do that right then, although logically any harvest of organs would have to be done quickly. I was not feeling particularly logical.

Michele kept relaying to me the questions being fired at her. After many minutes and many questions, I could no longer handle the request. They asked about every facet of Steve's life. I am sure they needed to know, but I was in no mood to carry on. Poor Michele was in the middle of that battle because I was getting fighting mad and wanted to be left alone. The calmness had subsided! The topper was one of the last questions: "Did he live in Germany during the '80s?"

Yes, we all lived in Germany during the '80s. The interview was over. Then came the explanation, "Stephen cannot donate. There was a mad cow disease outbreak there in the '80s, and we are not allowed to accept donated organs from people who lived there during that time!" What? After all that torture of rapid fire questions, he could not even donate. Why didn't they ask that question first instead of going through everything else and then asking the one thing that negated all the rest? I was empty of emotion! Numb!

We were still standing at Steve's side. I looked at him and could see he just was not there. His body was there, but somehow he looked empty. Very strange, I thought. I was glad he didn't hear us or see me getting so upset. The lid had just come off. I had not really tried to keep a lid on my demeanor. I was just going through the motions for the past three days, doing whatever was required minute by minute or hour by hour.

I had never really thought about what it would be like to lose Steve, even when he had been diagnosed with Parkinson's. Worrying unnecessarily about things I could not control had always seemed futile to me, and then we had talked at church about how worry was even a sin. We are to trust God. I thought about that, even though it was all I could do to stay focused on that trust. I felt so human, so weak, and so helpless. Now I could never lean on Steve again. I knew I was very blessed to have our daughters, especially leaning on them at that time, but Steve was my buddy, my partner, my lover, my friend, and my confidant. He was the only one in the world that knew me inside and out as well as another human being could. Besides, I had always tried to be there for my girls, so this situation would be such a new experience, leaning on them in time of crisis.

We were blessed with two exceptional daughters, who grew up to become strong professional achievers and, more importantly, loving and caring women of faith. Our older daughter, Michele, worked so hard to become a neonatologist (one of those doctors who cares for the very delicate babies born too early or with serious issues) and had married Jonathan, also a neonatologist. Her similarly dedicated sister, Terri, took another difficult path to become an attorney. She married Ken, also an attorney. How very happy these young ladies made their dad and me. We shared such pride in the women they became. Yes, they are smart and accomplished in colossal ways. But, they love Jesus, and they care about others. They are great mothers and (from our viewpoint), they are wonderful wives. We are proud of the people they became and the families they are raising. Between them, they have blessed our family with five grandchildren we love very much.

Steve really adored his daughters and grandchildren. He also had good relationships with our sons-in-law. All of this family closeness was very important to him, having lacked it with his family. He loved our family so much, and he was so proud of us all. Having a family that got along, wanted nothing from you, and shared love was his dream. It was his fairy tale! And he was happy to feel he could live it. His girls were close to him. He loved how they came to him for any advice about cars—his specialty above all. I was glad he had lived to know they were there. I kept thinking how fortunate that had been, tough as it was. I was glad they were there as I had to give the go-ahead to shut down life support. They had been so supportive, as much as they hated it, too. They helped me to think more clearly when I needed to the most.

8

Trusting God

*R*iding home with Terri allowed long hours of thinking because there was not much to talk about. We were shell shocked and had not been able to truly absorb what had happened. I briefly thought about the possible checklist of painful tasks that would be facing me to deal with this change in my life. How overwhelming. I had been a successful business woman and done many things on my own, but this was out of my range of knowledge. I hate being a planner by nature. Whatever happens, I go into autopilot fixer mode. I had no idea how to fix this.

Worse, I had such difficulty believing Steve was dead. I had traveled a great deal with work and Steve had done temporary duties that sometimes lasted several months. We had been apart at times. Just as retiring felt at first like we were on vacation, this new status of our marriage felt like Steve was off on a trip, and he would be home after a time. Thinking of him as dead was well beyond my ability to comprehend. I just could not believe it. I kept praying it was a horrific dream that I would just awaken to end.

Then in flashes of thought, it occurred to me how merciful God was. Steve had declared his fear of living out Parkinson's to the end as his dad had and how lucky he thought my dad had been by dying at a younger age with heart failure. Steve did not want to live through advanced Parkinson's. He was concerned about his own deteriorating body that would eventually fail him, but he was also fearful of becoming a burden. Jackie, his stepmother, had been homebound for several years, caring for his dad. She had wanted to do that and would not have had it any other way, but Steve did not want to put us through that. He had mentioned it to a few people over time, so it was a concern. He was a very personal person who would only talk to people he trusted about such deep topics.

I had assured him that we would deal with his condition as it came and that I married him for sickness and health. How blessed he had been to be so healthy until he got Parkinson's. The only answer had to be that God answered Steve's prayers with a quick fix—a car accident that ended his pain and suffering and prevented him from living his disease to the cruel end state. Suddenly, my head was filled with a new peace. Steve was with Jesus and would be taken care of now. He wouldn't hurt or worry anymore. My heart beat faster with a strange joy inside, knowing the love of my life was at peace. I hoped he was met by my folks and his dad.

Just as quickly, my heart thumped with sadness, jerking back to thoughts that I was not with Steve. I did not feel suicidal, but I had no problem thinking that God might take me with him. I hated the thought of being without Steve. So many things flipped through my catalog of things that would be hard or I would miss without Steve. Oh, how I wished I could shut down my brain. It was so tiring to think, think, think. I did not want to think!

Without skipping a beat, my thoughts shifted to how fragile love was because life is so fragile. One minute Steve was there, and the next he wasn't. It was just like the speaker had said at the July 4th celebration service. You could be driving home tonight and not make it to see tomorrow. Make sure Jesus knows you are a believer and you have a relationship with Him. Be saved if you aren't already. I thought how important it had been for Steve to walk to the front and pray with that man to recommit himself. He did believe, and he had become vocal about it. How comforting it was to know what he believed and how he felt about it. He was a good man, but most importantly he was a man of God. I felt more at ease thinking about that. How I loved that man.

I believed in Jesus since my youth and, although I grew up listening to a pastoral view of the Bible instead of digging into it myself, I felt a relationship with Jesus. I had never heard a voice speak to me, but I woke up many times with thoughts in my head that clearly came from a source other than me. God is good.

I thought about how perfectly our move to Tyler had been. We had planned to retire in Tallahassee, Florida someday. We liked the Florida lifestyle and weather but wanted a smaller town than Tampa with a less flat terrain. We were both working for the newly merged company of Verizon. Merging organizations meant reductions in force with great frequency. One day, a friend of mine called and asked if I was taking the new package offered to attract employees eligible for retirement. I had not paid attention, thinking I was not eligible. Moving with military transfers had left me with one goal—I wanted to be able to retire from *some* place. I had to change jobs so many times. She told me to check it out because she thought I was close. I had actually become eligible two months earlier! We were faced with a quick decision to accept the retirement package and decided to take it, thinking we would take our time moving whenever the house would sell. The housing market had been bleak, but we had no reason to rush.

We had a realtor meet us at our house. He convinced us that we should go ahead and list the house because the market was moving so slowly. We agreed. He put a sign in our yard two days later and was followed into the house by a buyer! Suddenly the whole plan changed. The buyer needed the house in three weeks — three weeks! I went to bed that night praying for answers. What should we do? I woke up the next morning with my head full of detailed answers. I looked at Steve and said, "I think we need to move to Tyler." "Tyler?" he asked. "Yes," I replied, "Terri is there, and it reminds me of Tallahassee." "You're right. I agree we should move to Tyler," he said. So, we called Terri to share our news and decisions. Fortunately, she was positive about our move. We agreed we would not try to move close to them so they wouldn't feel like we were trying to smother them.

So much for our plans. The property we wound up buying was next door to them. We had lived there for about six years when we had our accident. Thinking jobs would not be abundant in a smaller town, we were shocked when even jobs surfaced that could use our skills. We were there when my mother needed to move from Austin so we could care for her as she dealt with cancer and dementia. We were there when Terri had our special needs granddaughter. Living so close allowed us to be supportive. Circumstances pointed to a plan that fit everything together. We planned none of that. Each part of the move was perfect and timely. Now Steve had died, and I lived next door to my daughter. Only God could fit together such a perfect scenario.

If I had questioned anything about God before, I lost any hesitation with the string of coordinated solutions that just happened for us. I did not know why Steve was killed and I walked away. I had my theory that God answered his prayer, but I didn't know. I could only think that God had something left for me to do was why I did not die, too. I had felt God used me when I was in management to work for Him with a ministry of sorts, but I had retired now. Questions only left me going in circles. Nothing was making much sense. Wasn't the accident senseless? It did not matter. It did happen.

I had to trust God. He knew a lot more than I did, and I had to make myself stop churning the unanswerable questions. Hadn't God's plan worked out for us over jobs and moves when we trusted Him? I had no control anyway, but I needed to be obedient and pray for God to guide me. I prayed for peace. I prayed for Steve's peace.

When we got back to Tyler, we were limp with all energy drained from us. In some sense, three days had flown by, and yet it seemed long ago since Steve and I had started our trip. I was grateful to have two lawyers in the family to help me approach whatever legal stuff was coming. Besides lack of knowledge or experience with insurance, the accident occurred in Kentucky, the trucking company and driver were in Ohio, Steve died in Tennessee, and I lived in Texas. I knew I would need a lot of help, and I lived next door to that help. God was still on top of the plan. I had to trust God would take care of me.

Through all of the confusing and frustrating steps of dealing with those involved in the various states, everything *was* taken care of for me. I was required to sign appropriate papers after many calls and letters had crossed between my son-in-law and various authorities and lawyers representing the trucking company, insurance, hospitals, and emergency services. I was well taken care of and spared the tedious and painful negotiating and documenting. I was glad Steve and I had kept fairly decent records. I handled bills so I knew where account information was.

I could not imagine facing such trauma without faith. I could not have gone through the devastation without trusting God. I cannot imagine trying to figure out finances if I had never paid bills. I had been fully involved in our financial decisions and actions. Steve and I had taken turns paying bills, and we only had joint accounts so we both knew everything about our money. But dealing with all the details of the accident and getting it settled made my head hurt worse than it did from banging it. I knew from having been seriously injured when hit by the drunk decades earlier how complex and overbearing it could be dealing with all the veins of insurance filings and legal issues. But I had gotten through that with Steve. Now there were Ken and Terri, thankfully, so I did not have to go through that part alone. Ken was aggressive to get after it, starting by working right away to push for the death certificate. Having dealt with the deaths of my mother and father, I knew nothing could be done until we had official copies of that document. He was able to secure it from Tennessee sooner than I could have.

9

The New Normal

*M*ountains of planning and work needed attention. Fortunately for me, Steve was a "neat nick" so the house was its usual clean. Behind the scenes, so many people had become prayer warriors for us. Our Sunday Morning Bible Study friends and choir members started planning a meal to serve family and close friends who traveled to Tyler for Steve's service before we even knew when it would be. My daughters worked with me to plan the service for their dad and helped me greet loving friends who brought food to the house. People are so kind and caring just when you need them.

Of great importance was inclusion of the formal military funeral protocol. Military members came from Barksdale AFB, Louisiana to provide the military funeral with military uniforms, the flag, the 21-gun salute outside the church, and taps! We had a military wedding in honor of Steve's dedication to the Air Force and in honor of my dad. Men in uniform just look especially handsome and strong. I thought about how gorgeous he looked in his uniform. We had to have a picture of him in uniform at the funeral. We had one from the previous year because he had worn it to the July 4th celebration at our church, honoring the military each year. I was grateful we had that showing Steve's military pride in a current version. He was handsome, I thought.

The military element of the service provided a very special respect and honor to Steve—sentimental for all of us. Many people commented on how touched they were by the service. I felt sad and comforted when "It is Well with My Soul" was sung. That song had the answer. So many friends and associates came to pay respects. We did not have many family members left, but what we had of my family were there, including our daughters and their families, and my brother and his wife, as well as a few cousins. Steve's stepmom and stepbrother came from his family. I did not expect anyone else from his family, considering they did not go to his dad's funeral. None of us were surprised by the omission.

I was shocked, though, that some of those members of his family were spiteful enough to contact me and my daughters the night before Steve's service with venomous messages. I should have expected it, but I tried not to think about how other people deal with life. We never talked about them, but Steve had always warned that if something happened to him, I would hear from them. Sure enough, I did.

We had always kept our daughters out of the fray of his family. In fact, we had simply told them his mother and some others in his family were not nice, so we stayed away. Steve was adamant he never wanted to be around any of them again, and he did not want us around them. We agreed the hatefulness would end with us. Some people just have to find someone to blame for their unhappiness and keep things stirred up, I suppose. Needless to say, the girls were puzzled, and I was angry that anyone could be so cold on the night before their dad's service. Steve would have been furious! I wondered if he knew. I wondered if he saw everything from his new existence. I had to let it go. I couldn't let someone who meant nothing to me, and who Steve wanted nothing to do with, get me more upset than I was. We had quite enough ahead of us without wasting energy on people or things that didn't matter.

We managed to get through the day of Steve's service, feeling somewhat relieved to get it over with but at the same time appreciating all the people who honored him and us by coming. I had little strength to speak but wanted to share thoughts of my pride and love for my husband, so Ken graciously read my words for me. My brother also spoke a few words. Steve would have loved having them speak. Such respect was important to him. He had spoken at his dad's funeral as well as my dad's. He had flown to California for his mother's funeral, even though he had not seen her in years and had such a difficult relationship with her. Our preference was always to spend time with family while alive to appreciate them, but sometimes that was not possible. We always made every effort to honor services to show respect.

I believe many facts and feelings describing the good man Steve was were shared that day. People who might not have known learned of his love of Jesus, passion for Corvettes, love of country, and love of family. They did not even hear that day how Steve had been there for his dad, my dad, and my mom as they faced their own medical issues. He was modest about helping others even though he generously did so. He cared so much about his family. He wanted to move his stepmom to Tyler so he could be there for her and had initiated doing so, although he never realized that goal.

How special to see so many people there to comfort us and to acknowledge him. Steve may have been "just" a human man, but he was a very good one. I was overwhelmed, having never thought how many friends we had gained in so few years, and family coming from across the country. Of course, many people came for Ken and Terri, as well.

The attention given in the early days after such a loss are heartwarming and do help get you through it all. You have a focus and feel the love. How special to hear comments about how Steve had touched their lives and to hear fun memories. Under my black jacket, I wore a black Corvette shirt with sequined letters Steve had just bought me on our trip. Gary had driven down and was there for me again. Enough Corvettes were parked outside to have a car show. Steve would have loved that. Following that day, the beginning of my new life began with all of its challenges and pain.

When I returned to church and Sunday Morning Bible Study the next week, the lesson was about marriage. I could hardly sit there. Somehow I managed to get through the time, but wounds were stinging and my eyes were filling. We had sat in that class every week holding hands during prayers and being there together for a few years. Now, I was there alone. Singing in the choir was still of comfort, but Steve had loved the music so much that he even sat through our practices on Wednesday night. Now when I looked up to his usual spot—how empty. Looking down during church service to his front row pew—empty. The first weeks were difficult to sing without tears, but I was determined I had to hold it together and somehow I managed, even though many tears leaked through. Church was my comfort, especially the music. I loved the music worship. We shared so much there that I felt Steve there. Anyway, I still imagined him there in those empty spots where he had sat.

We had developed a habit of grocery shopping each week at a particular store, sometimes after church. Without him, visiting that store was beyond my ability. After years without him, some strange emptiness still fills me if I venture into that grocery. Consequently, even something as simple as shopping became a difficult task, and I had to start a new habit somewhere else alone. Until we moved to Tyler, shopping was the wifely thing to do, so I guess once he made it into a couple activity. I could not accept it without him in that store.

Grocery shopping was *our* thing there. I saw no reason to push the buttons that hurt.

Before the accident, I was committed to several committees for local organizations and volunteered at church. I managed to keep up with those commitments until the terms expired, but then I felt the need for a break. I did not feel like I fit that world any longer or that my heart was in it. My heart was not in much of anything except surviving each day with all that had happened over such a short time. I believe I was running on a sort of autopilot. My dad's voice was in my head again, telling me to carry on no matter what happened and somehow adapt. The world was going on, and it wasn't going to pick me up and fix things. I had to find a way. I was very blessed to have daughters and their families willing to carry me along, and I have never stopped feeling grateful for that. I know we have a special relationship.

I was a *widow*. Widow is a factual status of a woman that has lost her husband to death and has not remarried. That is, widow was a factual status until I was that woman and had lost my husband to death. I had a doctor's appointment about a month after my husband was killed as continuing care for my own injuries and for an annual exam. I was given the standard form to complete. Immediately following name was marital status. I froze. I stared at the paper. "Widow" was the fourth block following "married," "single," and "divorced." I had marked "married" for forty-four years. Marriage was my life as I trailed my husband where the Air Force sent him. Suddenly, reality smacked me broadside. I was a *widow*. What did that mean for me? My life was abruptly turned upside down, and I had no control. I felt like I was facing sunset, while my husband had just found the best-ever sunrise.

A cold chill bolted through my body, seeing that box marked "widow" for the first time. My shallow perceptions of what it represented gave that word negative power. My mother was the first widow I was close to, and she was in her late seventies before that title snatched her, following years of my dad's failing health and battling dementia herself. Although I had a neighbor about my age when I was in my early thirties who lost her husband to a heart attack, I never realized how being a widow really altered her life. She moved close to family almost immediately after the funeral because she desperately needed both financial and moral support, as well as assistance to care for four small children. Her reality seemed more like reading it in a book. I felt sad for her, but I had no idea how she felt.

But, this was *me* who was abruptly faced with being a widow. A *widow*!

Each milestone in our lives is personal to us, such as when we get married, when we have surgery or a major medical problem, and when we have babies. What mother thinks about everyone else when her baby is born? We live in the moment of our life—our event. Becoming a widow is no different. How we respond to this major upset in our life is very personal. This change is as personal as our marriage. Every marriage is unique because of the combination of the two individuals bringing it together. I viewed my marriage as a great one because we had lived through so much together and, in spite of obstacles and hard times, we had survived, feeling as excited about each other and our time together as we had when we met. We were not perfect but we felt perfect for each other. We believed we belonged together. I thought how very blessed I was that my last morning with Steve was filled with loving words and gestures. His last spoken words had been, "I love you!" in his last natural breath. I thought how tragic it would be to lose him had we been angry over something. No, my last memory of Steve is sweet, kind, loving, and happy.

As I fought to hang onto positive feelings and sweet memories, there it was—"Check appropriate box—Married—Single—Divorced—Widowed." How cold. Out of habit, I was about to mark "Married," but caught myself. "Single" sounded more gentle until I thought what that meant. Single would be someone never married. As harsh as the word "Widowed" sounded, that was what I was. Actually, without my prejudice about the word, what it represented was the best part of my life. I was married and had children with a special man who was now gone, not by choice. He had not rejected me. He was waiting for me in a better place, I thought. But he did exist and made my life worthwhile. The label began to soften in my mind, and I slowly allowed it into my vocabulary.

When the doctor entered, as soon as she asked why I was there, I started to weep. I could not contain my tears. With great compassion, she helped me to start realizing that my life would have to be taken one day at a time. I found myself weeping often and had no control over it. Her empathy was easily accepted, and I listened as she said out loud things I had been mulling over with resistance. No fix existed for this situation. A process was now underway that would take the rest of my life, no matter what other paths I might take. I would never have Steve back in this life, and I would miss him and our life together. That was reality. Death is quite final. We are not able to control the situation or go back. We have to go forward one step at a time. I had to go forward. I probably was not ready to hear that at that moment, but it stayed with me as I did start the process of grieving and healing. She convinced me that I should take some mild medication to help take the edge off of my weak emotional state. Medicine was something Steve and I both avoided, so I was hesitant, but I was glad I gave in once I tried it. We would try it for no more than six months.

While continuing treatment for accident hangovers, the time for my annual physical popped up. I had the annual mammogram and thought little of it. My girls were good about helping me get to various doctor appointments. Michele had moved in with two of my grandchildren in order to be there for her sister, with Laurel scheduled for the bone marrow transplant, and to support me. So much was happening at once that I really had little time to grieve. Then I received a call from the doctor's office. Something didn't look right on the mammogram. Are you kidding me? Now? I needed a biopsy, another traumatic experience I had not had. Waiting until after Thanksgiving for the results allowed plenty of distraction away from allowing depression to seep in as we anticipated Laurel's pending bone marrow transplant.

The family gathered together at our house for Thanksgiving, trying to carry on with old traditions. That day was so difficult for all of us. Steve loved Thanksgiving food and family. The day was empty without him, and his absence was magnified by efforts to gather where he was such a large part of the place. Everywhere you looked were little personal touches reminding me of him. We had things we had bought in Germany as well as his cowboy and car touches. He loved cowboys and wore boots and a cowboy hat at every opportunity. He used to tell me he thought he was born too late because he would have made a great cowboy. Hence, he loved Texas! I wished we had planned to eat out that day just to do something different. I learned that for me, trying to do things as we did them did not make me feel better.

We were all relieved by news after Thanksgiving, received a week before Laurel had to go to Dallas. The lab tests showed whatever had been removed during my biopsy was benign with surrounding tissue clear. Now we just had to get through Laurel's life-threatening issues. Simple! I could not believe the horrendous and frightening challenges my daughter and son-in-law faced having just lost Steve a few months earlier. Numbness is the only feeling I knew. I prayed and prayed to God for mercy to spare Laurel and keep us from losing her, too, when I was overcome with a strange reminder.

As freaky as it was, every time we had a new grandchild, we had just lost one of the older generation in our family. The trend started when our first grandchild was born and within two weeks Steve's dad had died. We had five grandchildren, and we had lost parents and a grandparent. We had laughed weakly at one point about who would be next if one of the girls got pregnant. With no more babies coming, it occurred to me that Laurel was having a totally new life of someone else's blood. She had to live. She was the new child for losing Steve. I know, my thoughts were pretty off the charts during this time, but I had to rationalize that Laurel would be alright.

Basically, my health was good with some inconveniences of headaches, back aches, and shoulder aches. Inconvenience was all it was. How very lucky (or protected) I had been concerning my own injuries. I tried to do as the doctor said, taking a day at a time and allowing myself to accept bad days as normal. I felt anything but normal. My body was there, going through the motions of eating and moving and driving. I didn't remember the actual accident, so driving was not unnerving to me. I didn't feel like I was in my body, though.

I don't know what an out-of-body experience is like, but my mind had not caught up with my body. I felt like a zombie much of the time, and it was not the medicine. Honestly, I wished I could just go to bed with the covers pulled up over my head and sleep all the time. However, I felt drawn to start Bible studies at church. I had done some, but now I needed to really focus on that because I was starting to feel depressed. I did not know how to deal with these feelings. Steve and I had been together since I was seventeen, most of my life. I moved out of my parents' house to our apartment. Now without warning, I was alone for the first time.

Friends were very kind and thoughtful. I felt so good having people around me who cared and wanted to be supportive, just as they had been about my granddaughter. Both daughters were right there, so I had people to help me. The problem was feeling alone in spite of those around. Until you experience this dilemma, understanding it is impossible. I learned that. This experience is so very personal. I had tried to be there for people I had known, not realizing the true depth of the pain and the severity of loneliness while surrounded by people.

People are awkward around you when they are not sure what to say. Some are nervous and try too hard. I know; I have felt like that myself. The most comforting people said little, but they acknowledged they understood and gave me insight to things that helped them cope. When too much is said, the hurt stings unintentionally. People said the typical things like, "He's in a better place," "He's better off," "You'll get through this," "You're so strong, you'll do fine," "You know they say losing a child is much worse," or "I know just how you feel." Really? I tried to be gracious through the comments, knowing the intention was to comfort. My comment was consistently, "Make sure your loved ones know how you feel always because life is fragile, and any minute could be your last. Steve knew he was deeply loved, and he made sure we knew how he loved us."

Comfort came from those few who had been through their own losses and simply looked me in the eye with an unstated message of, "I know," and gave me a hug. They did know. I treasured them. They expected nothing from me, and they were the ones who stood by long after the crowds left. Honestly, the first few weeks were busy with well-wishers and people bringing food and stopping by or calling. Then, it all stopped as quickly as it started. True friends remained and are still there. Sadly, I discovered a friend or two who appeared to do kind gestures to check off their good girl list but needed applause for every kind act. I was given some list of phases of grief that included anger, insisting I would go through that. It was inferred I had something wrong with me when I did not go through the anger phase. Another friend showed me later that it was twelve-step recovery that had actually been quoted. I was in a different recovery program.

People honestly wanted to help, but there is no cookbook for this.

If I learned anything, I learned to be more patient with myself. Many people have some concept for how a grieving person should act. Maybe I had my own that led me to compare to some imaginary list of traits or behaviors. I had to learn to let myself be myself. No right or wrong way exists for how to deal with a loss. Because we are all different and our circumstances are all unique, our way to deal with our situation will be our own, unlike anyone else's. We are usually hardest on ourselves.

I had been warned, you may lose a friend or two when you lose a partner. As if you aren't dealing with enough, you have to beware of people who use your grief for their own validation. Others simply don't know what to do with you. I knew divorced friends always said that, but I spoke to some widows who echoed that experience. There is nothing like being down and having an extra punch. I had to accept that some friends might be toxic and let that go. I had to realize I was in survival mode. You find out who your friends really are when you are alone.

Feeling lost, empty, and not knowing how to carry on, I turned to Bible studies. We had been going to church as "spectators." I had completed a few Bible studies, but those had been new experiences. Now I felt drawn to learn more about God's Word. At first, study filled a void of time. Then I found that filling my time learning about the Word started filling a worse void. Leaning on God's Word for comfort and learning to pray more frequently and deeper started to fill my well of aloneness. I still miss my precious husband so much. I long for the time when I will see him again. I may factually be a widow on earth, but I have relearned that I am first the bride of Christ as part of the church, filling a big void of being a widow! Jesus is always with me, giving me hope and lighting some of the darkness. It is a day at a time, but I do believe the image of "footprints" where He is carrying me when I need a lift.

The Bible studies did help me immensely for a couple of reasons. A very important impact was the need to leave the house and be around people in order to attend classes. Then focusing on the studies provided a positive theme. Attending class gave me some knowledge just by being there and listening. Homework gave me concentration on something bigger than myself. For me, the approach allowed me to float above the depths of depression, to which I felt vulnerable. I still would rather have stayed in bed, except for the fact that the house felt empty, even with family living there with me. Steve was not there.

Having been separated many times by our careers, I tried to think about how I managed during those times. Those times were usually awful because, without fail, anything on the verge of breaking waited until he was gone. As if on cue, the sprinkler system broke not long after I got home from Tennessee. I had no idea where the controls for a second unit he had installed were, so I could not even turn off the spewing water. And this time, I knew he wasn't coming home. How I wished he would walk through the front door.

I knew I would not replace the destroyed Corvette. Cars were *his* hobby. I realized how much I had invested myself into his hobby and lost track of my own. I could not even say what my hobby might be anymore. As much as I enjoyed sharing it with him, I had no skills to delicately care for a new Corvette and no interest in continuing our Corvette life by myself. We also had two other cars that he enjoyed tinkering with and keeping pristine. Walking into the garage and seeing them was such a painful reminder that I decided to trade them in on one car that I hoped I could manage. Steve and I had talked about getting a Cadillac CTS, so I set my sights on trading in two cars for that one. Several people reminded me of the advice not to make any major decisions for a year. But, I could not see those cars in the garage for a year, and I didn't want to keep up two cars, anyway. Steve always did any dealing on cars, of course, so Terri helped me get through that event. I bought a new CTS. I rather liked it and was pleased with myself that Steve had said that should be our next car.

The new car had only had a home in my garage for a very short time when I had a disturbing dream. Steve was right there in front of me asking, "When are you going to replace the Corvette?" I said, "I am not going to replace the Corvette." He asked again a few times then asked, "Why did you buy a CTS?" I replied, "You said that should be our next car and that you really liked them." I woke up almost sitting in bed, expecting Steve to be sitting there, but he wasn't. What a crazy dream—except it felt like he was right there. I could feel him, or so I thought. I couldn't tell what was real anymore. The whole accident still seemed like nothing but a nightmare, and I wanted to wake up from that awful dream! I wished I could go back to sleep and keep talking to him in my real dream.

When I could not stand to walk into the closet, I decided I had to go through Steve's things. His neatness made the task physically easy but emotionally draining. I would smell his clothes, trying to get some brief whiff of him. He was a military guy to the core—everything smelled starched, fresh and clean, just like him. The two sinks in the bathroom were hurtful to see. I found myself uncomfortable going in there.

Having sons-in-law that Steve liked and who I knew would appreciate his things provided some comfort as I sorted through Steve's clothes and boots. They liked some boots and clothes and seemed eager to take what they could use. I gathered up some other things, hoping to one day have one or both of the grandsons excited to have them and donated the rest. Knowing Steve's love of Corvettes and appreciation of the museum, I boxed up his collector Corvette model cars to donate to the museum, along with old car magazines. He would love that, I thought. I could imagine him grinning at me, working so hard while fussing over his collection. I loved that man, so I loved those Corvettes.

Sleeping had not been so difficult once I was home. I wasn't agonizing about his crumpled state as I had been at the hospital. I hated admitting that I actually slept more soundly without his snoring. I hated to admit it because I would really love to hear him snore again, I thought. I had told my daughters how I wished he was there to aggravate me. I missed everything about him—the touches, the smells, the voice, the laugh, the looks, and even the snores. I could not comprehend never cuddling on the sofa or holding hands during prayers or driving the highways or enjoying retirement as we had dreamed it. And I loved how he would scratch my back! He knew just what I liked. He had recently been on a kick of making milkshakes, and I wanted one.

10

The Accident

So many details still had to be handled following the accident. The paperwork was incredible. Death highlights just how involved the government is in our lives. We should all have stock in paper, even with the amount of work now done electronically. I had a huge briefcase full of all the necessary documents, especially because Steve was in the military. You have to prove everything. Thankfully, Steve was organized and kept everything. I could put my hands right on what was needed. Even so, I spent days sorting it all out to make sure I could check off the list.

Ken handled all of the calls and letters requesting accident documents for insurance. He negotiated with everyone to make the best settlement. Some friends asked if I was going to sue. I would not have even been so aggressive to settle the insurance if Ken had not been there to handle it. Steve and I did not believe in the "sue attitude." Too many people immediately sue to get whatever they can. Accidents happen. We did not get an attorney when the drunk hit me until a year later when the insurance company said they would not cover my medical any longer. With Ken and Terri, both attorneys, I had great advice readily available that I could trust. They agreed we needed to negotiate the insurance settlement and not just take what they offered. I am grateful for that.

Ken was dealing with the insurance companies, hospital, EMTs, and police and was successfully able to resolve the business. Suing would not do anything but raise blood pressure. Money was needed to pay enormous emergency and hospital bills, but money could not recover a person. Money cannot hold my hand. My main job was to heal myself and do what I could to support my granddaughter's upcoming bone marrow transplant, as well as be with Michele and her kids. Ken worked through the legalese of four states for nine months before the accident claims were finally settled. At the same time, he and Terri worked full-time and prepared for Laurel's torturous procedures. The bone marrow transplant required several months of isolation at Children's Hospital in Dallas, where Terri would live in the cramped room with her. We and Ken's family would supplement where we could to provide support.

Michele stayed for about five months with two of her children. They very sweetly helped lift my spirits by putting up a Christmas tree and doing what decorating we had that year. Jonathan came with their other son for Christmas, and we all stayed in a Dallas hotel. Our first Christmas without Steve was spent in the hospital, taking turns being able to see Laurel, who received her new bone marrow a week before Christmas, following ten days of extreme chemo. What a miraculous gift she received in the bone marrow of a most special young lady who turned out to be her donor. She was a very delicate and sick little girl but always the one with such a sweet nature. How cute and touching the way she would thank the nurses after they administered some painful treatment. It was so gripping to see all she endured in that little five-year-old body.

I missed Steve so much, but I didn't have time to grieve that first Christmas or my birthday the following month.

Laurel had grave complications following the transplant and wound up in ICU. For a couple of weeks, everyone was hovering around the hospital. We lost a dear son of my cousin and his wife but missed the funeral because Laurel came so close to passing away herself that day. My brother and his wife had stopped by Children's Hospital on their way to the funeral and decided to stay with our family—a very thought-filled gesture. We got through that, and Laurel continued her bumpy recovery followed by a careful and protective year, praying she would not reject her new bone marrow. Thankfully, she did make it through that very rough year. With all of the focus on Laurel, none of us had the energy to really grieve. My observation is that we often have multiple tragedies that occur in close proximity to each other. Perhaps God protects us from falling into uncontrollable grief by keeping us confused with diversions. I know my mind whirled with so many major activities that I didn't have time to feel devastated all the time. I felt an odd peace. I felt guilty when I had a fairly good day—you know, one of those when no one added a crisis, major or minor.

As if we lacked things to divert our attentions, Ken, Terri, and I decided to find a house where we could all live together. Yes, we started deciding this while Laurel was in the midst of so much critical activity. I did not want to stay in our house. We had it built, so it was what we liked, but without Steve it was just a house. Having moved so many times in my life, I never became attached to a place or things. I could hear my dad in my head, reminding me how we had to be ready to move on and adjust to new adventures in our lives. Consequently, *things* were not important to me. Oh, I had things I enjoyed that I might be upset to lose, but I soon got over it unless it held some sentimental value.

Steve and I had been talking about selling our house and buying a condo, so I soon decided I wanted to go ahead with that plan. I wanted to sell the house and buy a condo. My state of mind had already reached move ready. We had planned to buy two condos. We had spoken to a realtor when we were in Florida a few months earlier, and we were pondering where we would like to have a home part of the year. We missed certain things about Florida when we moved to Texas, even though we loved Texas. Upkeep of house and yard were getting more challenging for Steve, so he was ready to have no maintenance.

I decided that upkeep on a house and yard were beyond my desire, especially without him. Soon I discovered many tasks beyond my awareness. I tried to tell Steve how I appreciated the things he did, but not until he was gone did I discover the special things he did about which I had no idea. Steve loved being outside and so enjoyed doing yard work. I could only tolerate so much of that and with Steve being such a handyman, I was at a loss for where to start with many repair and upkeep tasks, inside or out. It was no great surprise that I desired a very low-maintenance residence. When I told Ken that I wanted to go ahead with a condo, he said, "No you aren't." He said he and Terri had already talked about it, and they thought we should find a house together. He then noted that the Bible says you should take care of widows. Wow! I did not have to think about it very long because I did feel close to them, and we did get along well living next door. I did pray and think about it, though, as I know they must have, long and hard. I was so humbled by the offer but so excited. I really never perceived any downside to it. Not only would I have a home to share, but I could be there to help with Laurel. We could help each other.

After a good bit of house hunting with a realtor, we all agreed upon a house we thought might work. We liked it enough to call in an architect who drew up some plans to remodel existing space with a second master suite. As we prepared to sign the contract, the house was being inspected. Halt! The inspection was being done on the first day rain had fallen for months. The half basement had a leak. The foundation had serious issues. The inspector did not even complete his inspection. How fortunate we had not signed that contract. How fortunate it rained that day. The rain reminded me of how our move from Tampa to Tyler had worked out so well, as though someone planned it. I only know of one who has the power to make rain.

We had to start over with house listings. As incredible as it sounded, Terri looked online and was drawn to a listing that was not in Tyler and did not list the extra living space but had a floor plan displayed. The house had two master bedrooms! We made an appointment to see it and were amazed how well it fit what we had outlined. The second master had a bath with one sink—actually, a lovely space with mirrors angled around the sink over a large counter space. A very large shower without a tub was next on my list of wants. This bath was great. The house was a one story, better for an aging person like me and for delicate Laurel, which was incredible!

The house was brand new, never lived in, and was built with great style, many upgrades, and very good taste. We all loved the house. The only hesitation was the location outside of Tyler. I was retired, but Ken and Terri still had to commute to work. They agreed they liked the quiet area, and it was worth the drive. The drive seemed reasonable to me because we had usually lived at least ten miles from work, as this was. They were used to living closer. And so my life started over, living with my daughter and her family.

Some people have rolled their eyes and commented how they could not imagine living with their kids. I think our living arrangement works because we have respectful love. We allow each other space. We don't share every meal together or sit around together every evening. I have a lovely master bedroom with plenty of space in a peaceful setting. I feel comfortable in the whole house, but I enjoy my room, my personal space. I don't have a mother-in-law suite with my own kitchen or anything like that. We have one kitchen and dining room and office and utility room. We share it all as any family might. Of course, being retired, I have freedom to do laundry when they are at work and do that. I could eat with them every night, if they were able to sit and eat together every night. With growing girls, too many evening activities like church and dance and school prevent everyone from being together at the same time many nights. When we are all home, I generally choose to dine in my room and allow Terri and Ken to enjoy their girls as they would have if I still lived next door. Having that special exclusive parent time is so important that I have no desire to infringe on that space.

Doesn't that leave me alone? Yes, it does. But, I can tell you that I remain alone as far as the life I was accustomed to, no matter who is around. My husband is gone. It's funny when I think about it. My mother tried to convince me, when we moved all the time and I was sad about leaving friends, that I had her and my dad so I wasn't alone. I explained to her that she and my dad always had each other, but I was alone when we moved. There is no bond like a married couple with a good relationship. I don't try to compare losses with anyone. I have not lost a child, although we certainly felt close during Laurel's traumatic scares. As a mom, I always felt so responsible for my children and needed to protect them and loved them so dearly but differently than I loved Steve. I have no sense that allows me to even desire to compare losses, and I respect the description of those who have shared their feelings of their experiences. Any time we lose a loved one, we are faced with such unbearable pain that it is indescribable. Nothing prepares you to know how to cope, just as little prepares you for raising a child with their individual personalities and quirks.

We were enjoying the new house, I was keeping Laurel during the day, and we were selling our houses that first summer. I kept my bedroom furniture and a few special things but sold the rest or donated it. It was all just "stuff" now that Steve was gone. I didn't need it, and I have similar tastes to Terri, so we managed well. I fixed my bedroom with several mementos and pictures of Steve. I could look at them and maybe have an occasional chat with them. I was getting along well, and Laurel was steadily improving. I missed Steve a lot, but I was coping. I felt like I was adjusting.

One morning, I was waking up when I had the strangest experience. I was lying on my side cuddled up to my pillow with my hands cupped around it when I felt Steve lying behind me; his body fit snuggly right against my every curve and his arm wrapped over me just like he used to do. My mind was frozen. This felt so real I could not move for a long time. I did not want the feeling to end. If it was a dream, it was the most real, wonderful-feeling dream I have ever experienced. I felt like Steve was there. I could feel him cuddling me. When I finally got up, I could not shake that feeling. The whole day I was captivated by the thought of that morning. I know I missed him and wished things would be different, but can the mind be that strong? I didn't care what it was. I felt like Steve had been there, and it made me feel good. How I wished it would not end.

Meanwhile, Ken had dealt with the legal issues for me. I did not see the car after the accident. Ken saw the pictures taken at the scene and later but did not think I needed to see them. I did not care to see them. I never remembered anything about the actual accident beyond seeing that guardrail coming at us. I had no memory of hitting it or what followed. I did not realize our car had flipped on that guardrail, ripping the top right off. Even when I regained consciousness, I was sitting in a car with no top and could not comprehend that I was sitting in the open air.

In fact, I knew little about the car until a year later when Michele and Terri returned to the museum with me to see a memorial bench honoring their dad. Gary met us, graciously hosting our visit, allowing us to enjoy a tour of the museum and sharing lunch with us. Our eyes filled and overflowed when we saw Steve's bench neatly placed on the path of memorial benches. Tears were shed in pride for a wonderful husband and dad as well as sadness from missing him.

Steve and I had seen the little memorial park a few months before our accident when we had last visited the museum. Steve had been very touched by them, especially seeing a few that had recognition of Christian faith, military service, and a love of Corvettes. I knew he would be honored by such a gesture. We had decided to plan on a memorial bench shortly after the accident but were amazed at how friends donated to help us fund it. Steve had a few good friends in Tyler with the local Corvette club and had gained many friends across the country through a registry website formed for new and potential buyers of the new Grand Sport model we had just purchased. With his knowledge of cars, especially Corvettes, he had learned all he could about the new model before we got ours and was eager to share everything he knew with other enthusiasts.

When people from the local club and the Grand Sport registry learned of our accident, I was flooded by prayers lifted for us and kind thoughts and offers of help, as well as money they donated for the bench. I was speechless, learning that so many people who had never met Steve personally respected and appreciated him so much and called him friend. One group from Virginia sent me a prayer shawl along with a sweet note explaining how the group prayed for us while making the shawl. We had met many Christian Corvette lovers in our travels and on caravan trips, but I had no idea how sincere these people were about following Jesus until I felt their support for us. Contrary to what some people think, Corvette people tend to be more conservative, religious, safe-driving citizens. They love their cars and love to go fast, but they don't go crazy. Most fast driving is on tracks where events are held. Safety is always promoted and enforced when caravans travel.

Gary talked about how special the Corvette "family" had been when Steve died. Word had spread rapidly, especially because a caravan was expecting us to be with them. As we enjoyed looking at the memorial bench, we talked about how Steve would love the cross in the middle, Air Force insignia that covered one side, and the Corvette on the other. His life was captured by birth and death dates and a quote, "Driving with the Angels Now."

Gary asked if I had ever seen the car after the accident. I told him Ken had taken care of the settlement and thoughtfully shielded me from that. Gary shared conversations he had had with Steve when Steve told him he had Parkinson's and how his dad and my dad died so differently. He shared his anxiety about living out the disease and being a burden to family, especially me. Gary knew we were Christians as he was.

Steve had added the roll bar to the car because he liked the stiffer, more stable feel of the car with that addition. I had complained about it a bit because I could not move my seat as far back due to the necessary placement of the bar. Steve had said if I didn't like it after that trip, he would have it removed, so it became a little inside joke between us. Well, Gary mentioned that bar and I told him how I had complained. He understood my complaint but went on to tell me what he saw when he looked at the car.

Gary said, "When I looked at the car, I saw the hand of God on it. The roll bar was flattened on his side and shoved into a perfect halo around your head!" Chills ran through me. God was there, no doubt! Several people had commented that a guardian angel had to have wrapped me up to have Steve so hurt sitting inches away and for me to walk away with a sprained shoulder. I think the seatbelt probably caused my injury while it saved my life. Because the car flipped on the guardrail, the airbags did not deploy, which sometimes cause injury. The bumper did not hit to set them off. The top was gone, and the windshield bent in toward us, totally shattered. Blood was visibly splattered, but none of it was mine. The emergency team believed I had to be seriously injured as they looked where I was sitting. That was why they insisted I could not move as they lifted me out on a board.

Gary also pointed out the spot where our car hit, noting that had it hit five feet sooner, the car would have gone off the road into a field. Because Corvettes are so low and wide, the typical result of going off the road into that field would have been to spin around out there. Instead, we hit the guardrail. Steve's life was taken as a matter of about five feet difference. A coincidence like that is beyond human imagination. The only answer to the why of that result is God in my thinking. I agree with Gary's feeling that God's hand was on that. I believe God's hand was all over this. Steve prayed to pass more like my dad than his, and ultimately, his heart could not sustain him on its own—like my dad.

I had comforted myself with thoughts of Steve praying to not live out Parkinson's, by believing God's plan was to take him before his symptoms escalated further. How I wished the time had been years later, but I knew only God's plan mattered. Gary made a comment about me surviving as I did because God must have something else for me to do. Some purpose for my life was still to come. I believe everyone does have a purpose, but I have struggled to define mine. Nothing spectacular had come from my time on earth that I could see. But the more I studied the Bible and worked on my own relationship with Jesus, I felt the skewed sight I must have had for what God values. We humans tend to value visible, tangible, eye-popping actions, especially in a day of so much spectacular technology. I became more confident that God is the only one I need to obey and please. I decided to listen more intently for Him and stop being drawn to artificial standards of culture and society.

The trip to Bowling Green provided some closure for me and I hoped for our daughters. Gary helped me to confirm what I thought I already knew about the "why" that I refused to ask. Accidents happen. Our accident seemed to be part of a bigger plan. Survivor guilt was diminished by that visit. I had dreaded going back to where my life was so abruptly wrecked. As it turned out, the visit allowed some finality and freedom to let go. God was with us—that was clear. Not being a fatalist, I don't carry on, carelessly thinking what will happen will happen, but I do believe God knows all of our choices of free will and knows the ending of each story even when we make choices not in his plan. I do believe God took care of Steve and me, in a strange turn that somehow incorporated a truck driver with no ill intent. I still wonder about him and pray for him. How difficult it must be to know a simple action resulted in someone's death! Because we settled only with the insurance, and I signed release statements not to further pursue any litigation, it is hurtful that the driver or company could not see fit to send me some note of condolence. But, I understand how the laws make such actions impossible to expect.

One recurring thought about that day was why we were on that highway that morning. We had been in Bowling Green a day earlier, so we had time to visit the museum and for Steve to exchange a car accessory he had bought on our previous trip. When we left the hotel the previous morning, Steve had gone through town, the route he had chosen on our last trip when we stayed at that hotel. For some reason, he decided to go the other way and take the highway that day. I thought it odd, but there was no reason to question his path. We could go either way. Of course, it occurred to me that had we taken our usual path, the truck driver would not have been there! But, what difference did it make? We did take the highway and the truck driver was there! I knew I could go crazy trying to critique it all. (Business habits are habits but not good for this.)

Even more disturbing was my memory of looking at a big tanker truck as we passed it on our way to Bowling Green. We were driving through Tennessee at the time. As I sat there, for some reason I looked at the huge tire outside my window and had a horrible thought of how awful it would be for a Corvette to hit one of those tires. Thinking back on that was too eerie. I had no idea why I thought that and never told Steve. I had time to think all kinds of things on long road trips. But that thought came back to haunt me.

11

Therapy

Steve and I had planned an Alaskan cruise with Jackie. I asked her to go ahead with the trip as planned over his birthday that next May. She agreed to go. We had a very good time, although it was not without some sensitive moments, considering Alaska was one place Steve had wanted to see. How I missed him. How we missed him. Being around the time of his birthday, I was glad we were having a new adventure, seeing new things, and spending time together. We had been close since we first met when Steve got back with his dad. We had a common thread of surviving the antics of Steve's mother, and we often talked for hours—kind of like free therapy.

While on that cruise, I thought about how I had spent Steve's last birthday—his 65th. The 65th birthday was a big deal to him. Most birthdays had not been of great interest to him, but that one was. We had planned to spend two weeks in Florida, specifically at the Disney complexes. While living in Florida, we had annual passes and enjoyed going to Epcot most months just to walk around the lake and see some shows and eat. We lived close enough to drive over there just for an afternoon. Our girls wanted to surprise their dad for his birthday so planned with me to join us the week of his birthday. He was surprised, actually, shocked! He was very happy. We had not spent time with just our girls since they left home. We loved being with their families, but there was something special about having just the four of us together for that week.

When Steve first saw them, he whispered in my ear, "I thought we were here to have fun, you know!" He was kidding — kind of. He was thrilled that his girls cared enough to fly to Orlando to be with him and share his special birthday. We had a great time, and it meant so much to him. I thought how perfect that we had that time together less than three months before he died.

After the Alaskan cruise with Jackie, I stayed home to care for Laurel. Perhaps as resolve from years of moving, I had an urge to go someplace once Laurel was recovering well. I decided to take advantage of a Christian study trip to London through our church. I invited Karen, my doctorate study friend from Kentucky. Steve died a month after I finished my doctorate so she went to my graduation with me and then joined me for the London trip. Focused on Christian history, we became absorbed in each sight and activity. We met several very nice ladies, who happened to be widows. We had a good time, but Karen later said how different I was — subdued, I suppose.

Nancy, one of the ladies I met, was a sweet, fun soul who led the Sunday Morning Bible Study for widows at our church. I recognized an opportunity for me to change Sunday classes and be with women who shared my new life phase. The more I got to know them, the more I determined the need to join that group. When I got home, I did exactly that. These ladies each had their own unique, tragic story of how they lost their husband and the difficulties they faced alone. Having someone to talk to who understood so much of how I felt, even though their experience was quite different, provided an emotional home for me. They not only met for Bible study but they made a point of having frequent social gatherings, if only to meet at a restaurant for lunch or dinner. I began to fill one of my voids. Having a safe environment where you can share if you need to or just listen is important. Listening to other women talk about their situations and families also helped soften the pain I felt, hearing how young some of the husbands were and some of the difficulties the ladies had to deal with. How could I not appreciate that Steve and I lived through such a long marriage and had a full history to reflect on. I had so many wonderful memories to hold dear.

When study topics were sensitive, this group was able to tailor it to their situation, so marriage discussions with this group were safe. We did not whine and complain but rather supported each other, listened to each other, and laughed with each other a lot. Everything was put into the perspective of finding comfort through the Word and believing God wanted us to have joy in all things. We all missed our spouses and needed to hold on to the Bible for answers. I found right away that one of the biggest voids in my life was not having Steve to talk to and share life with. I have my kids, and we talk, but it is not talk like you have with a spouse. At every turn, I just wanted to pick up the phone and call Steve. We all had that void. Oh, how I wished I knew the number for Heaven!

The decision to join this group of widows for my Sunday morning fellowship was the best thing I could have done. I love my family so much and love living with my daughter and her family more than words can express, but unless you have lost a husband, you are not able to understand the loss as one who has. People can be all around you, so technically you are not alone, but inside you always feel alone. As much as I treasured the short time when Michele and her kids lived with me, that time was so foggy because of Steve and Laurel! We had so much going on. I know they were the reason I actually had a Christmas tree and felt some joy. But you feel like a fifth wheel no matter what you do around people. Anyway, that was how I felt. I was used to having a partner who knew me to do things with and just be with. We spoke on a totally different level. Our looks alone could say volumes.

I do enjoy travel, but it is very different without Steve. With your spouse, you just know what you both like and more easily decide what you will do and where you will go and when. With someone new, you start all over with discovery to find the best way to do something as simple as who likes to shower when. Second nature no longer works. Gone is taking anything for granted. Inside jokes haven't developed. History can't be shared. No one understands unless they live it. And even if you live it, you can't understand the unique situation of another.

What I learned most from this group of ladies was the need to love Jesus more than ever and have joy in my every walk. I found confirmation that God's Word is true, and we will be provided for. With extreme appreciation, I realized just how well I had been provided for. My daughters were there for me when I needed them, and I knew they always would be. Above all, Terri and Ken had accepted me into the core of their family, and Michele's family offered to have me with them. I did not have to live alone as most of my widow friends did, even when they were close to their families. I belonged to a family every day. I did not go home alone. Even if they were gone, I lived with a family, so I did not go home to an empty house. Even our little dogs got along! I had a Yorkshire terrier, and Terri had a toy poodle that were best buds when we lived next door, so there was little adjustment there.

I discovered, as my new widow friends had predicted, that it was actually successive years following my loss when it became harder to cope. The first year, especially for me with so many other crises, was numbness. I was sleepwalking through the days and activities. I suppose I was bandaging myself in some protective fog to feel less. I was also taking the mild medication to "take the edge off." I believe that was a kind way to help me through the toughest days.

Once I gained more confidence about my new life, I began to feel the need to start fresh for my own wellbeing. That was when I became closer to church, volunteered more there, and removed myself from old committees. I enjoyed my work with all of those community groups, but I associated my time with them as part of my life with Steve. Losing Steve left me feeling a strange emptiness inside, and I realized that the answer for me was to find a new "normal." I was building a strong relationship with these new widow friends. I trusted them and found a place where laughing and sharing could be done safely. They did not make me feel like they were watching me, judging my recovery, or feeling sorry for me. I had some bad days, but I had new, understanding friends who were there to cheer me on to appreciate more good days.

I looked for opportunities to find myself and escape, I suppose. The next big trip was a mission trip to Turkey. Karen invited me on that trip. We made some new friends and felt an appreciation for the simplicity and beauty of people hearing the gospel for the first time and accepting Christ. My heart was opening up to a new place. I hungered to learn more. I had grown up being told what to think and what the Bible meant in formal, traditional church services. Now, I was more eager to read and explore for myself.

I took more Bible study classes and became engaged in a special study group of women that planned a trip to Israel. I invited Michele and Terri to go with me. Michele was able to take the time off and did the trip with me. Having Michele as my roommate was comforting. I didn't have Steve, but I was with our daughter, and it was just the two of us. I say that because it is different when I am with the whole family and my daughters are with their husbands. I do feel alone and intrusive to some degree in those settings. It is called reality.

Both of us were overcome with the depth of feelings at being in Israel, at those sites we read about in the Bible, especially having the verses read as we stood in such incredible places. My strength was returning, and I was learning how to listen more to God's words and less to negative thoughts passing through my mind.

I was going to make it through this new life, and I knew it, able to endure through the lonely and painful days. Steve and I were learning Christians, growing in our faith, but having faith. I was continuing to grow as I learned more and learned to actually trust.

> *Surely God is my salvation; I will trust and not be afraid. The Lord, the Lord himself, is my strength and my defense; he has become my salvation. (Isaiah 12:2)*

I thought how hopeless it must feel to not have faith, not to believe in Christ. With my new widow friends, I had discovered one strong similarity. We all believed in Christ and felt peace about where our husbands were. We had hope. Visiting Israel only strengthened my faith and belief about everlasting life. How fruitless would life be if it ended at death and nothing existed after this life. Especially with Steve gone, I wanted to find my way closer to Jesus. Our widow group agreed on that as we all experienced our personal loss.

I felt humbled, hearing the stories of other women, their lives, and their losses. Many had lost their parents, as I had, before they lost their husband. Each loss was different because of individual relationships and circumstances. Listening to stories of long illnesses requiring extensive care reminded me of Steve's dad and how tough his shrinking health had been. I thought how I had anticipated taking care of Steve and then how he had died so abruptly instead. No loss is easy, but I felt very fortunate that I believed Steve was in Heaven and was not in pain or suffering.

I thought how before these ladies helped me see my new life as still worthwhile, I felt jealous that Steve was safe and at peace and I was left. I had to force myself to remember that guilty feelings would get me nowhere and I should not feel guilty, as the doctor had warned. I never felt suicidal, but I did feel quite ready should God decide he wanted me, too. Life had a different feel to me with the void I felt. My energy was waning. Strangely, I had the sense of how precious life was and the need to love openly at the same time I felt unneeded. These feelings were more factual than whining.

Over time, I had many episodes where the tears felt like they were building up and might explode, but I could not cry. I found myself watching chick flicks with tender, sweet stories that made me cry. Shedding those tears sounded silly, but the experience left me feeling relieved, so I would periodically find a movie when the need to release surfaced. I guess we all have to find what works for us in any stressful or painful situation. No one judged my approach in our group. Rather they respected my need to find a way to deal with this new life.

Travel serves as my outlet for escape three or four times a year. I enjoy the trips and the wonderful sites each time. My memories of the trips are sketchy, although with each one, I get better about accepting life without Steve. Nothing changes the fact that I am a widow. I liked having a husband, with all of the good and the irritating sides of it. I loved Steve. We both knew we found the love of our life in each other. We were able to accept each other as our imperfect selves.

12

What Now?

Each year has had its own impact on my life. Each year comes with better acceptance of this phase of my life. Yes, the daily habits and activities become more normal. The people you can rely upon remain steady. Real friends have remained after the first year or so. New traditions start, and travel can bring excitement to an otherwise dull time. Yet, without warning, some little thing can hit you with a gripping memory or feeling that is swift, like a kick in the gut. You have to just roll with it.

The house I bought with Terri and Ken is on a small lake, and we added a great pool. Looking at it some days makes me think how Steve would have loved this. Then it dawns on me that we would never have lived here if he was alive. A Corvette drives by, and I think how he would appreciate seeing it, especially if it is well cared for. A movie reminds me of the way he would say something or an actor he liked comes on. After all our years together, so many things remind me of him. How sad he cannot see our grandkids growing up. Or does he see it? I don't know. I have often almost reached for my cellphone to call him out of reflex. I hope he is somehow aware of the goodness in our lives. I am sure he knows even more than we do that God is good all the time. In spite of these trying years, I do see that God is good and surely loves me and my family.

As I cuddle with Belle, my Yorkshire terrier, I am reminded of Steve's sweetness. We liked dogs and usually had one or two. Steve's best friend German shepherd died shortly before we moved to Tyler in 2003. We still had our Yorkshire terrier, Buddy. We went to Utah to spend Christmas with Jackie in 2008. She had recently lost her dog and wanted to look for a new pet. Upon arriving at the pet store, we noticed a petting area with some small puppies, two of them Yorkshire terriers. Steve went over to them and called me over. I told him, "Don't pick them up!" Well, he did pick one up and handed it to me. She immediately snuggled right into my neck. I was doomed. I said, "No, we came for Jackie. We have to get back to Texas and can't get a dog." He put the puppy back, and we agreed we would go back to Jackie's.

As you might imagine, we thought about and talked about that adorable, sweet puppy most of the night. Jackie had not found a dog she wanted. We agreed to go back and see if the Yorkshire terrier was still there in the morning. She was, and we did buy the precious puppy we named Belle, after the Disney character. Our granddaughters were pleased about that. Steve just wanted me to have her and talked me into it. Now I am so thankful he did. Our other Yorkshire terrier died about a year later, but when Steve died, I had Belle. We had no plans to get a dog when we got her! Another coincidence? Belle is of great comfort to me, and helps me reflect on some of the sweetest times.

In our years together, we were blessed with a truly good life. We were so proud of our daughters and their families and loved them so much. How special to share a life with all that. We were successful, getting each other through college and supporting the ensuing, rewarding careers we had. We did it together, just as we had dreamed. But we agreed many times that our greatest achievements—maybe our main purposes—in this life were having two beautiful daughters who have strong faith and strive to care for others. With God's love, we replaced ourselves with better people than ourselves. I don't know what tomorrow brings. I do know one of the best things that happened for Steve was the moment he heard another veteran speak about making sure Jesus knows you by acknowledging Him, because you never know when your time will come. I think about that often. Steve and I had been baptized, and I know he had faith, but that recommitment was so comforting for me. I don't know when I will see Steve again, but I do try every day to work on my relationship with Jesus so that I can be with Him.

Widows are special women, mentioned in the Bible. God cares about us. God cares about me. A guardian angel had to have been with me at our accident. One must have been with Steve, too. He must have been in pain, but most of his body went numb. I find that merciful. If he was not going to survive, how precious that he was able to have time to see his girls, without feeling his broken body. He was on medication, but from the time of the accident, he never seemed frantic. His only question was if it was his fault, and I am so glad that Gary told him it was not, and I was able to tell him a truck hit us. So, Steve knew it was not his fault. That was important to him.

A few people have suggested to me that one day I will meet someone else. People seem to worry about you if you don't have a husband. Maybe that will happen, but after five years alone, being a widow is alright with me. I don't *need* a man. My belief is that if you just want to get married, you can find someone. I am not looking. I miss having a guy to share dinner or a movie with and good conversation. Men are great. I like them. But that doesn't mean I need one. I had a great partner and remain thankful for the many years we were blessed to share and the family we were able to enjoy.

I am even grateful for the ups and downs of years filled with the challenges we faced. We got through everything together. We grew in our faith together. Nothing was more rewarding than that.

I have found that my widow friends are wonderfully understanding, have no expectations of me, and are fun people. We have caught the attention of those around us by our uncontrollable laughing. During one such episode, Nancy replied to a comment about how much fun we were obviously having, that we were the "merry widows!" Laughter erupted all around us at that comment. Laughter is good medicine. Maybe a laugh a day keeps depression away.

I am not equipped to counsel anyone else, but I have learned how to survive and pick myself up again. We each have to find our own way to deal with obstacles in our lives. Many more wait for me, I feel confident. Some changes will be positive. One such change happened for me when Jackie, Steve's stepmom, decided to move to Tyler and be close to us. She has been my friend since Michele was just a few years old. We have always had a special bond and respect for each other. She is a mentor who I have always looked up to, and now she is here. Steve was very fond of Jackie, and we had hoped to move her close years ago. She understood the injustices and hatefulness he had grown up with and appreciated his ability to overcome it with a peaceful and kind demeanor. We were both collateral damage from "wars" Steve and his dad had against Steve's mother. We understand because we both married men severely damaged by her. She comforts me, and I feel good that I can be there for her. She has been a widow for many years with much grace. She is a wonderful example of surviving and living by putting others first. I want to live like that.

My home situation is unique, but it works for me and my family. I love being able to live with my daughter and her family and have my stepmother-in-law right here. I know

Steve would find it optimal and be happy for me. The situation is a little close for some people, but I guess the respect we have for each other coupled with love is enough. I have also enjoyed traveling and spending time with Michele and her family. My world is full and very blessed.

We were so sad that Michele lived in New York, so far away. How can you possibly be as close to grandchildren that you see infrequently, only when you are visiting? Sharing some of the daily living of kids makes the dynamic so much better. I know the other grandparents miss the granddaughters we had here just as we missed our New York grandkids. How great it would be if whole families could join together again and at least live fairly close to each other.

I guess a serious problem with our world is how jealousy and hatefulness have existed since the first brothers on earth. Humans can't seem to fix that. We couldn't even fix it in our extended families! I find it sad that we are unable to have strong relationships with all family, but conflicts within families are fairly common. Steve and I always agreed to protect our family against negative influences, whenever possible. Life has enough turbulence without engaging in it. Being part of a sandwich generation (in between parents and children at the same time) the benefits of having family close is magnified. When family members need help of any kind, how much easier it is if you live in close proximity. Steve and I wanted to have that closeness with our family. That is why we moved to Tyler. We really liked Tyler, but Terri lived here. We lived next door with mutual sharing and helping. We could be there for each other. That was priceless. (And the weather in East Texas is not bad!)

13

Final Home

More than anything, I see that I rely even more on Jesus as my comforter and hope. It is Jesus I want to please without the divided attention to please my husband. My life was devoted to pleasing Steve (most of the time!). I believe God has us formally say vows of marriage before Him because He wants us to be devoted to each other and become one within Him in His Heaven on earth. Being human, our capacity to maintain our first devotion to Him is challenged when we have someone we love dearly that we have also made a covenant with. I know that I often struggled with that balance, even once Steve and I began to learn more and work toward keeping the Lord first. I loved Steve so much, and I could touch him, so he was in my range of thoughts and attention.

I don't know why part of life has to be the pain of losing those we love to death, even though I have read rational explanations in commentaries on the Bible. One thing I do believe is that losing them to death means they have everlasting life in God's Heaven if they have accepted God's grace. I take great comfort in knowing my parents and husband accepted and acknowledged Jesus. I expect to see them again one day because I also believe in the one way to eternal life. What a joyful day that will be! We met when we were individuals with God, then we were united together with God, and then we again were individuals with God when Steve died.

> *At the resurrection people will neither marry nor be given in marriage; they will be like angels in heaven. (Matthew 22:30)*

When first I heard the scriptures talking about marriage not existing in Heaven, the thought was disturbing. I loved being married to Steve. I want to be married to Steve forever. However, thinking of being in Heaven without the evil of this earthly world and instead having the magnificent love we will know there with everyone focused on praising God, the beauty of Steve knowing me and welcoming me without needing the vows required by limited earthly corruption is exciting to ponder. Heaven on earth has so many incredible places and creations that imagining the pure beauty and perfection of Heaven is beyond my human conception.

I find comfort imagining my time with Steve in Heaven. Our pastor has described our Heavenly life as busy, not sitting around on clouds all day. I like that. I imagine singing most of the day, praising our Lord in indescribable harmonies and worshiping all day no matter what else we do. Steve didn't sing on earth, but I hope he will be singing with me in Heaven. I can visualize Steve and me in Heavenly "cars" riding around and enjoying unbelievable beauty of sights and sounds so beyond anything we can even imagine. My greatest dream would be for us to drive in caravans of "cars" loaded with our dearest family and friends, Jesus in the lead, hearing unimaginably beautiful music. Imagine!

Ultimately, we are all ending this life at some point and going somewhere. Heaven is my choice. Going as a widow is okay with me because all labels will disappear once we pass through the "gates." Nothing of this life will matter then. Steve could not take his precious Corvette with him. In fact, his precious Corvette "died," too. Money he worked so hard to earn, education he worked so hard to earn, the cars he worked so hard to perfect—nothing went with him. I plan to follow one day and reunite, but until I join him in our final home, I plan to be a widow of pride and integrity to serve our Lord as best I can. We had a joining of hearts under God, until death did we part. Half of our marriage heart has gone ahead to Heaven. Before he left this earth, we were able to leave each other with our last words, "I love you!" No one could create a better caption for the picture of our life. Yes, I have been living the sunset of our life together, but I look forward to joining Steve in the Heavenly sunrise.

Steve, until I see you again, *I Love You.* Jan

14

Serenity Prayer

he Sunday Morning Bible Class for Women Redefined (widows) started each Sunday with the Serenity Prayer. Nancy, the leader of that group, began with that prayer because it said how we needed to live to survive our new normal. None of us wanted to be widows. None of us were educated or prepared to deal with our individual situation. Every death in a family has its personal footprint. Every family dynamic is unique. We have to choose to deal with our new life and find a way to understand who we are in our new path. Time does not "heal" the pain, from my experience. But we do somehow adapt to this most difficult turn in our life over time. We cannot control everything in our lives. We can learn to accept challenges and remain steady with trust through our faith. We need to live one day at a time.

Serenity Prayer*
Reinhold Niebuhr (1892–1971)
God grant me the serenity
to accept the things I cannot change;
courage to change the things I can;
and wisdom to know the difference.

Living one day at a time;
enjoying one moment at a time;
accepting hardships as the pathway to peace;
taking, as He did, this sinful world
as it is, not as I would have it,
trusting that He will make all things right
if I surrender to His will;
that I may be reasonably happy in this life
and supremely happy with Him
forever in the next.
Amen

*The Serenity Prayer was written by Reinhold Niebuhr, an American theologian, for a sermon at Heath Evangelical Union Church in Heath, Massachusetts in 1934. Niebuhr's sermons and church groups spread the prayer through the 1930s and 1940s. First published in a magazine column in 1951, the prayer was popularized by twelve-step programs. Several versions have evolved based on the original.